ADVANCE PRAISE FOR
THE GREAT GATSBY COOKBOOK

"This book is the 'Cat's Pajamas'...the 'Bee's Knees'...and just makes me want to have a party! It's got everything you need to throw a quintessential Great Gatsby Gala including cocktails, menus, recipes, prep lists, advice on how to dress, what music to play, and what vintage movies will set the mood."

—**Gale Gand**, pastry chef, author, Food Network host, James Beard Award winner

"*The Great Gatsby Cookbook* is beyond a cookbook—it's a party in itself! Cristina and Ron have created an entire world. They have combined amazing recipes with history and literature, as well as fashion, music, and movies. A night at home? Throw on a tux or fringe dress, put on some hot jazz, and sip a cool Gatsby-inspired Gin Fizz. Or invite friends over to celebrate. Wow them with cocktails such as a Gin Rickey and Mint Julep, plus dishes like Jellied Beet Bouillon, Welsh Rarebit, Five-Course Sandwiches, and desserts such as Strawberry Bavarian Cream, as well as a fantastic Speakeasy menu. This book has everything you need!"

—**Virginia Bell**, former New York City restaurant owner and author of *Midlife Is Not a Crisis: Using Astrology to Thrive in the Second Half of Life*

"As with every other cookbook Ron has written, this collaboration with Cristina is destined to amaze! His dishes are complex in depth, flavor, and texture, and accessible to the home cook. The theme here is one of pure celebration! Well done and well timed! Bravo! Looking forward to creating an event around these recipes!"

—**Michelle Ciccarelli Lerach**, founder of Berry Good Night and Berry Good Food, executive producer of Kiss the Ground, and Disciple of Escoffier International

"*The Great Gatsby Cookbook* is the perfect gift for the entertainer in your life! More than your average cookbook, inside are delicious recipes developed from classic dishes and drinks of the 1920s with a modern twist and a wealth of background information. From an afternoon tea to a formal gala, this guide will help you throw a '20s party for a group of any size with everything you need to plan each event—fabulous food, costumes, music, movie, and decorating ideas. For those who love food, drink, entertaining, literature or history, it's the bee's knees!"

—**Valerie Costa**, Food and Drink Editor, *The Union*

"Cristina Smith and Ron Oliver's *The Great Gatsby Cookbook* is a delight from beginning to end. Yes, it's an excellent cookbook, but also a step back in time to the world of Jay Gatsby and friends. Taking cues from the pages of Fitzgerald's great novel, it gives us a chance to relive that exciting and dangerous period in American history: the Roaring Twenties. Highly recommended!"

—**Dr. Russell Fanelli**, Professor Emeritus, Western New England University

"*The Great Gatsby Cookbook* is a beautiful reflection of the Roaring '20s. Its unique approach takes you back to a period of prosperity, art deco, fashion, and cultural revolution. This beautiful book combines stories, anecdotes, cuisine, and cocktails studded with lightness and humor. Vive les Année Folles!"

—**Bernard Guillas**, Master French Chef and award-winning co-author of *Flying Pans: Two Chefs, One World*

"'Ain't we got fun...' *The Great Gatsby Cookbook* is just that and way too fabulous! What a joyful trip to the 1920s and its life and times! Cristina and Ron have got the party covered as well as teatime, the Ladies Lunch, the Gala dinner, and even the Speakeasy—get down with all that jazz! Wonderful recipes, amazing cocktails, and such a deep insight into a huge transformational time in American History. A cookbook like no other, this is a perfect gift to yourself as well as everyone on your gift list! Bravo! Cheers! Well done!"

—**Darity Wesley**, author of *You Can Transform Your Life* and *How to Be the REAL You*

"Our community, along with hundreds of our guests and program participants, has enjoyed Cristina's magical relationship with food for many years. Watching her in the kitchen is like watching a miracle happening. We also have Cristina to thank for connecting us with Chef Ron Oliver and the pleasure of his food magic as well. Their collaboration has created a book unlike any 'cookbook' I have ever seen. Let the parties begin!"

—**Ingrid Coffin**, founder of Blue Sky Ranch community and retreat center

"Whether she is cooking for two people or a hundred, Cristina Smith is a master chef. After a quarter century of eating what she cooks at my retreat programs, I am still mystified by the magic she creates. The culinary opulence and joy of the age of *The Great Gatsby* lives on in these pages with Cristina and Ron's brilliant collaboration. I'd better cook one of these recipes soon, or I might just eat the book!"

—**Steven Forrest**, author of *The Inner Sky*

"Cheers to the chefs! *The Great Gatsby Cookbook* is a must-own, step-by-step glam guide for fabulous retro entertaining. It provides the reader with festive recipes, decor inspiration, and a guide to bubbly—plus an enticing bird's eye view of the man himself. It even provides a fashion overview so that everyone will be dressed to a T! As a Champagne Girl with a very discerning palate, I adore this full immersion joie de vivre experience...even the playlist is spot on! Put on your boas and pearls, girls, and let's toast to your next entertainment success!"

—**Mary Giuseffi**, fashion model and consultant; author of *Undeniably You! The Good, the Bad and the Fabulous!*

"Très bien!"

"This book is like a party in a box—everything you need for a successful event!"

THE

GREAT GATSBY

COOKBOOK

FIVE FABULOUS ROARING 20s PARTIES

CRISTINA SMITH

CHEF RON OLIVER

Post Hill
PRESS

A POST HILL PRESS BOOK

The Great Gatsby Cookbook:
Five Fabulous Roaring '20s Parties
© 2021 by Post Hill Press
All Rights Reserved

ISBN: 978-1-63758-103-2
ISBN (eBook): 978-1-63758-104-9

Cover art by Cody Corcoran
Interior food photographs by Marshall Williams
Interior design and composition by Greg Johnson, Textbook Perfect
Art Deco border illustration 185769028 © Oleksiy Makhalov
Measurement Conversion Chart illustration 210507520 © Viktoriia Ablohina

This book contains information relating to the health benefits of certain ingredients. It should be used to supplement rather than replace the advice of your doctor or another trained health professional. All efforts have been made to ensure the accuracy of the information in this book as of the date of publication.

Post Hill Press
New York • Nashville
posthillpress.com

Published in the United States of America
1 2 3 4 5 6 7 8 9 10
Printed in Canada

HERE'S TO YOUR HEALTH AND HAPPINESS!

CONTENTS

Roaring Twenties Movies and Music

ALPHABETICAL RECIPE LIST

THE ROARING TWENTIES

ARE YOU READY TO PARTY LIKE IT'S THE 1920s?

The decade of the 1920s was one of the great party periods of the twentieth century—and that's saying a lot! It was a wild time of innovation, change, drama, inequality, Prohibition, music, and dance.

There was plenty to celebrate. World War I and the Spanish Flu pandemic were over. Women were voting and claiming their power in many realms of society. Some expressed it through fashion as *flappers* by bobbing their hair and wearing mini-dresses, sometimes with lots of sparkly beading, feathers, and fringe. Movies hit the scene, making the big time and dazzling people around the world. Music was bursting with brilliant innovations like radio, records, and jazz. Forbidden liquor was served at *speakeasies*, which required someone in the know and a secret password.

People were migrating from rural areas to the cities. In the 1920s, a new sense of individualism developed for many, leading to the passionate pursuit of pleasure and enjoyment. New love, new music, new dances, and new fashion were all fueled by a new outlook of optimism. People were changing and shifting traditional gender roles, since women had entered the workplace at wartime, and there was more time for leisure due to technological advances for the home. Cars and airplanes were becoming more common.

Technology, science, the arts, and business were innovating rapidly, producing tremendous advances and inspiring inventions. Some of these breakthroughs radically changed society and set the stage for where we are now.

Cuisine, fashion, music, and entertaining were reaching new heights of the sublime and the outrageous, and everywhere in between.

Literature was blossoming as well. The literary scene of the 1920s included brilliant authors like F. Scott Fitzgerald, Ernest Hemingway, Gertrude Stein, Langston Hughes, Edith Wharton, T.S. Eliot, Colette, and

e. e. cummings. The world was introduced to *The Great Gatsby, Ulysses, Lady Chatterley's Lover,* Agatha Christie's super sleuths, *Winnie the Pooh,* and *The Velveteen Rabbit. The Great Gatsby* was a high society selfie of the times. Fitzgerald introduces us to the parties, the music, the casual inequality, the excess, the heartbreak, and the stunning transformation of life as he knew it.

Fitzgerald was a brilliant and original writer. His personal life was glamorous, tumultuous, obsessive, tragic, and frustrating. It was filled with extremes, alcohol, and personality conflicts that could overshadow his creative genius. An icon of the times, Fitzgerald lived and wrote about the high life while battling inner demons. He came from wealth but struggled financially to support himself and his family. His wife, Zelda, was diagnosed with schizophrenia.

Regardless of personal challenge and tragedy, Fitzgerald could write. His style is lyrical and resonant. He doesn't just say that *a breeze blew the curtains.* Instead, he says:

> *A breeze blew through the room, blew curtains in at one end and out the other like pale flags, twisting them up toward the frosted wedding-cake of the ceiling, and then rippled over the wine-colored rug, making a shadow on it as wind does on the sea.*

The Great Gatsby was written and published in 1925 and set in 1922. It got some good reviews, but it didn't sell much until the year after Fitzgerald's death (1941), when the book was reissued by the publisher. *The Great Gatsby* then began to be appreciated by scholars and teachers and was declared a classic. Now it is one of the most widely read novels written by a twentieth-century American author.

Fitzgerald's writing style in *The Great Gatsby* is conversational; as readers, we feel as if we are talking with a friend. His main character elicits our sympathy and compassion, even as we are shocked and appalled by the behaviors and attitudes of some of the others he describes. His voice is dispassionate. He portrays the excess, the alcohol, and the casual assumption of superiority and entitlement by the wealthy while giving us an insightful snapshot of what the Roaring '20s roared about.

I was within and without, simultaneously enchanted and repelled by the inexhaustible variety of life.

Entertaining is certainly one of the elements of the social change that made the '20s roar. People were ready to party big time, to celebrate. The economy was booming. Household appliances, like the vacuum cleaner, washing machine, and refrigerator, made domestic life substantially easier. Cuisine advanced due to the game-changing benefits of a freezer and refrigerator over an ice box. Because shopping didn't have to be done daily anymore, food could be prepared in advance. Frozen, out-of-season, and non-local ingredients were available for the first time.

If you were one of the people or knew one of the people who raked in the dough as the economy changed post-war and post-pandemic, there were events happening all the time once you got into the circuit. Word would go out about a party, and those in the know just showed up, no formal invitation necessary. Some of these were massive, permissive, rave-like parties featuring dancing, drinking, festivities, and band after band all night long, sometimes for days.

Opportunities to entertain and be entertained abounded. Tea, high or otherwise, a-la-the-'20s, the well-appointed ladies' luncheon, and the as-formal-as-you-want it sit-down dinner were all on the menu. The diner-like food you might get at a speakeasy introduced Italian and other cuisines to the American palate. The glorious variety of small bites/appetizers to titillate the taste buds and stimulate the senses were grazed upon at a more casual party. These often opulent occasions were enjoyed by party goers wearing glad rags designed to dazzle the eyes and accompanied by magical music to set the mood.

Everyone was ready to cut loose, and they did it with vigor and enthusiasm, regardless of social status. The newly rich and the old money hosted many a gala party. Flappers, scrappers, jazzers, and razzmatazzers knew how to celebrate with whatever they had. And baby, they knew how to eat, and we are going to take you there! This book will give you everything you need to put on the perfect theme event. From a fun family dinner to a full out gala, we will take you step-by-step into the world of 1920s-style entertaining blended with the savvy, technology, and variety of today.

Award-winning chef Ron Oliver has taken fifty-one of the most popular, exciting, and interesting recipes of the 1920s and updated them for the modern palate. Incorporating current ingredients and food sensibilities, these mouth-watering dishes range from simple and delicious to intricate and show-stopping.

This book will show you how to have fun entertaining with a 1920s flair. Feel free to use these recipes in any combination you wish. The recipes range from quick and easy to exotic with multiple elements. No need to use the entire menu for any given party. Pick and choose whatever is right for your special occasion, skill set, and energy level.

This appetizing, full-flavor spectrum cookbook of classic American cuisine features:

- Five fun 1920s-themed parties complete with recipes and step-by-step instruction to make putting together any size event as low-stress as possible
- Recipes for eight that are easily adjusted up or down
- Cocktail recipes and a guide to champagne and bubbly
- Quotes from *The Great Gatsby* generously sprinkled throughout in italics
- 1920s movies, music, and fashion tips, plus fun facts about the times

Now—*let's get this party started!*

THE GOODS ON GATSBY:
THE MAN, THE MYTH, THE LEGEND

Have you ever met *The Great Gatsby*? Some read it in high school or college, others were captivated by seeing one of the many movie versions. Maybe this is your first encounter. Besides all the great party descriptions and rich writing, there are actually some themes addressed that are very familiar to us today. Social inequality; the excess, entitlement, and often unconscious privilege of wealth, and racism are present. Also revealed are the dangers of obsession and the tragedies that can happen when we focus on the fantasy of another person. These are laid bare for exploration in Fitzgerald's amazing and timeless classic. Going beyond the lyrical language, exquisite word portraits, and all of the juicy, jazzy fun stuff, there are core elements to the story line that are somewhat disturbing and thoroughly thought provoking.

Throughout the book there was much speculation about Jay Gatsby. Where did he come from? How did he make his obviously considerable wealth? Was he a bootlegger? A gangster? He clearly had *gonnegtions,* but to what? Or whom? No one seemed to know, and Gatsby wasn't telling.

We are lured in through the eyes and experiences of Nick Carraway, the man next door. He's somewhat inept and a bit confused, but fascinated by Jay Gatsby, his glamorous and stylish neighbor, and all the endless parties and delights he hosts. Nick is invited to attend these galas, and he does so, giving us a fly-on-the-wall-type report, sharing his insights to all the goings-on.

> *The last swimmers have come in from the beach and are now dressing upstairs; the cars from New York are parked five deep in the drive, and already the halls and salons and verandas are gaudy with primary colors, and hair shorn in strange new ways, and shawls beyond the dreams of Castile.*

We are introduced to Nick's cousin Daisy, who is married to the extremely wealthy Tom, an old college buddy of our narrator. Beautiful, vain, self-indulgent, and often bored, Daisy is at the heart of the story and root of the tragedy in this casually sordid tale of delusion and obsession.

> "She's got an indiscreet voice," I remarked. "It's full of—" I hesitated. "Her voice is full of money," he said suddenly. That was it. I'd never understood before. It was full of money—that was the inexhaustible charm that rose and fell in it, the jingle of it, the cymbals' song of it.

Spoiler Alert!

After many parties and adventures, we discover late in the book that Gatsby knew Daisy way back when and had carried a torch for her ever since. A torch that didn't sputter and go out when she married Tom. That flame burned so hot that it motivated plain old James Gatz, son of unsuccessful farm people, to imagine and give birth to the Great Gatsby in order to find and woo this woman of his dreams. He built the Gatsby myth, piece-by-piece, by means fair and foul. The times allowed the foul means to include rum running, gangsters, and the mob, but we only get hints of all those underground connections. Gatsby carefully crafted, cultivated, and curated his charm and charisma.

> He smiled understandingly—much more than understandingly. It was one of those rare smiles with a quality of eternal reassurance in it, that you may come across four or five times in life. It faced—or seemed to face—the whole external world for an instant, and then concentrated on you with an irresistible prejudice in your favor. It understood you just so far as you wanted to be understood, believed in you as you would like to believe in yourself, and assured you that it had precisely the impression of you that, at your best, you hoped to convey. Precisely at the point it vanished...

Gatsby arranges a fateful reunion with Daisy through Nick, and reveals himself and their past over tea and lemon cake. Rekindled sparks fly.

His heart beat faster and faster as Daisy's white face came up to his own. He knew that when he kissed this girl, and forever wed his unutterable visions to her perishable breath, his mind would never romp again like the mind of God. So he waited, listening for a moment longer to the tuning-fork that had been struck upon a star. Then he kissed her. At his lips' touch she blossomed for him like a flower and the incarnation was complete.

Later, in epic Shakespearean-tragedy fashion, Daisy ends up killing the woman her husband is having an affair with in a hit-and-run accident driving Gatsby's car while drunk. The victim's husband is encouraged (by two-timing Tom) to see Gatsby as the perpetrator and ends up killing Gatsby then himself.

Daisy and her privileged husband barely miss a beat and return to their decadent lives, slightly bored, and look for the next great party. Meanwhile, Gatsby's funeral is attended only by our narrator and a few others. The fair-weather friends have flown the coup; the illegal collaborators don't want the association. If there's no advantage to them or party to be had, no one else is interested, just Gatsby's heartbroken but proud papa and Nick. Not a happy ending.

These vivid views and visions of the best and worst of the Roaring '20s linger in the imagination, long after the character names have fled. And Fitzgerald's inspired writing is downright haunting, old sport.

If personality is an unbroken series of successful gestures, then there was something gorgeous about him, some heightened sensitivity to the promises of life…it was an extraordinary gift for hope, a romantic readiness such as I have never found in any other person and which it is not likely I shall ever find again.

THE 1920s PALATE

There was a food revolution during the '20s in the United States. What people ate and how they dined underwent a total transformation. Diets shifted dramatically from eating primarily meat and potatoes to include more fruits, vegetables, and dairy. Americans became more health conscious and eating raw vegetables became trendy, especially lettuce, tomatoes, and celery.

It was the beginning of the health food movement, vitamins were discovered, and the science of nutrition was born. *Diet & Health* was the bestselling nonfiction book of 1922, which is the year in which *The Great Gatsby* is set.

> *Every Friday five crates of oranges and lemons arrived from a fruiterer in New York—every Monday these same oranges and lemons left his back door in a pyramid of pulpless halves.*

New flavors were introduced by immigrants to the cities, both from far across the ocean and the rural areas. An expanded variety of food beyond what was locally grown was cheap and plentiful. Advances in refrigerated storage and transportation provided access to food that might otherwise not be in season, making fresh fruits, vegetables, and fruit juices available all year long.

This created a complete culinary paradigm shift which enabled people to eat healthier and spend less time cooking food from scratch. Newly introduced pre-prepped foods dramatically reduced preparation time, such as peeling, cutting, shredding, soaking, and grinding. Convenience was king, and the popularity of canned foods increased dramatically after safer production methods were introduced. Ready-to-cook food, including frozen foods courtesy of Clarence Birdseye, were all the rage.

Electric and gas ranges with a stovetop and oven were a game-changing innovation, replacing coal and wood-burning stoves. Electric refrigerators replaced ice boxes and the freezer was introduced. The first home freezers cost more than a car!

Labor-saving kitchen devices like the mixer, blender, and toaster were introduced and quickly became essential. And the ultimate means of comparison for an awesome kitchen advancement, sliced bread, made its debut. Now we understand the expression "the best thing since sliced bread!"

Refrigeration and freezing meant perishable food items could be stored for much longer. People no longer needed to tend to a garden or chop wood for the stove. Countless hours were saved by not having to spend as much time pickling, curing, and canning in order to store food without refrigeration. Cookbooks became popular, allowing people to expand their culinary horizons at home. Many of them were geared towards entertaining, instructing people how to be the perfect host—including proper service and structure.

What did people do with all of that time they saved? They entertained and partied!

INVOKING FORBIDDEN SPIRITS

One of the touchstones of this fabulous party decade was that alcohol was illegal in the United States for all but the first sixteen days of it. There was a great societal obsession with alcohol, whether you were pro or con. It became a powerful forbidden spirit with a compelling allure that was let out of the bottle like a genie. It helped define the era. Prohibition made it illegal to manufacture, transport, or sell alcohol, but it was perfectly legal to drink it—it was just *crackers*!

Craftily enough, there were legal loopholes available, like getting a prescription for medical alcohol and medicinal liquor. You were allowed to make up to two hundred gallons of wine and cider from fruit at home. Grape growers and vineyards sold crushed grape concentrate with a warning label. It let consumers know that by following certain steps, wine would be made. (Don't try this at home! Wink, wink.)

A whole underground economy for bootleg liquor boomed. It was the beginning of the booze cruise. Underground clubs and drinking establishments, *speakeasies*, popped up everywhere. They were famous for patrons needing to whisper the password or show a membership card in order to gain entry. "Speak easy" came from the instruction to speak quietly so as not to be heard by the police. A number of speakeasies had secret entrances.

The clubs themselves varied from large upscale establishments with jazz bands and elaborate ballroom dance floors to small dingy backrooms, basements, and tiny rooms inside apartments. At the peak of the era, there were estimated to be upwards of one hundred thousand speakeasies in New York City alone. Black musicians, Italian wine makers, liberated women, people of all genders and sexual preferences, writers, artists, inventors, thought leaders, high society out for a thrill, politicians, and opportunistic entrepreneurs on both sides of the law all mingled freely.

A number of speakeasies had secret entrances.

Mixed drinks and cocktails became popular, mostly as a way to disguise the taste of poorly made distilled whiskey or *bathtub gin*. This opened up a whole new realm of mixology, creating some of the drinks we still love today. Cocktail parties as an entertaining genre emerged as a more private way to socialize over a drink.

Great Gatsby-Inspired Beverages

COCKTAILS AND BUBBLY DRINKS

Parties start with drinks. It's just the way things are done, whether during the 1920s or today. We all need a little social lubrication. For your own version of '20s-themed drinks for pre-dinner socializing, or a cocktail party with delicious delights to nibble on, here are some suggestions. They range from straight up classic alcohol-based adult beverages to fun, bubbly, sparkling drinks the whole family can enjoy. Here's to you, old sport. Cheers!

> *The bar is in full swing, and floating rounds of cocktails permeate the garden outside, until the air is alive with chatter and laughter, and casual innuendo and introductions forgotten on the spot, and enthusiastic meetings between women who never knew each other's names.*

All About the Bubbly

Champagne is everywhere throughout *The Great Gatsby*. You can get a little light-headed just reading the book.

> *In his blue gardens men and girls came and went like moths among the whisperings and the champagne and the stars.*

> *...champagne was served in glasses bigger than finger bowls.*

In spite of Prohibition, at least according to the '20s portrayed in *The Great Gatsby*, drinks of all kinds were everywhere, and the champagne flowed like a river.

The term *champagne* is most correctly used to describe the effervescent wine that comes from the Champagne region in France, but common usage has most of us calling any bubbly wine champagne. *Prosecco* is the term used for sparkling Italian wine.

What is it about bubbles that brings us so much joy? Whether it's the magic of blowing soap bubbles as a child or the effervescence of champagne and other bubbly drinks, there is fun, celebration, and delight contained within those bubbles. Many of us shout or exclaim at the first sound of popping corks, or at the small explosion that opening sparkling water or club soda makes. The party is on!

These days there are lovely options in the bubbly department that are non-alcoholic, from sparkling cider in various flavors, to effervescent mineral water, to plain old club soda if you want to add some jazz to fruit juice. Presentation is everything. Find the right glasses. A champagne flute is long, tall, and lean. A champagne coupe tends to be shorter, rounder, and curvy. Many vintage, thrift, and ninety-nine-cent stores carry inexpensive glasses that can be just the ticket, especially if you want to offer your guests a pastiche of potables to taste.

There are some confusing terms that are used around champagne (most correctly called sparkling wine if we are speaking of a California or other American vintage). There is a scale of *dryness* that describes the level of sweetness of the wine. Paradoxically, *Extra Dry* is the sweetest, followed by *Brut*, which is considered dry. And then there's *Extra Brut*, which is considered drier yet. Dry or sweet literally describes how much sugar is in the wine. The drier it is, the less sugar it contains. *Blanc de Blancs* is made exclusively from white grapes; *Blanc de Noirs* is a white sparkling wine made from red grapes. How dry or sweet you like your wine is a matter of personal taste.

Champagne also now comes in colors. Rosé champagne—okay, sparkling wine—is now available at all price points and levels of sweetness. The color comes from the natural pigmentation of red grapes that is added to the finished wine. It used to be the case that all pink champagne was very sweet, but that is no longer true. Many of the modern rosé sparkling wines are quite dry *and* quite delightful!

I was enjoying myself. I had taken two finger bowls of champagne and the scene had changed before my eyes into something significant, elemental and profound.

Any '20s party worth its salt needs to include champagne and other bubbly drinks. There are so many choices. Let your personal taste and preferences be your guide. You might have to do some (imbibing) research! Oh, darn!

Don't forget the lovely non-alcoholic options. The days when sparkling apple juice was the only champagne alternative are long over. Just in that arena there's sparkling white grape, pomegranate, cherry, all kinds of apple combinations, and there's even a variety of organic choices. More research! This is a project the kids can help with!

Sparkling waters of all kinds come in various flavors and presentations and can be added to simple juice to make it bubble. Using juices can add to your color palate for even more fun and splash.

You can also add juice to a bit of champagne if you want to play with color and taste. The days when orange juice was all that was added to champagne to make mimosas are long gone. Now there's cranberry, watermelon, blackberry, and mango—and the list goes on endlessly!

Consider the food you're serving and the vibe you want. No need to get carried away unless you really want to! A few bottles of sparkling wine of your preference and some sparkling something non-alcoholic will get your party off to a delightful start. There's one main, significant, and very important rule to remember: have fun!

Cheers!

Gin Rickey

A refreshing adult beverage for a hot summer day.

   3 ounces gin
   1 ounce freshly-squeezed lime juice
   3 ounces club soda
   2 lime wedges

Add gin and lime juice to a highball glass. Add 6 ice cubes. Gently pour in club soda. Stir once. Garnish with the lime wedges.

Tom came back, preceding four gin rickeys that clicked full of ice. Gatsby took up his drink. "They certainly look cool," he said.

Gin Fizz

The Gin Fizz is basically a Gin Rickey with a few twists and turns. A bit of sugar is added, and it is shaken, then strained. It is also common to add egg white to fizzes to give them a frothy foam on top.

½ **tablespoon superfine sugar**

1 **ounce freshly-squeezed lemon juice**

3 **ounces gin**

1 **raw egg white**

3 **ounces club soda**

Add sugar and lemon juice to a cocktail shaker. Stir to dissolve sugar. Add gin and egg white. Place top of shaker on. Shake vigorously for 15 seconds. Add 8 ice cubes. Shake vigorously for 10 seconds. Strain into Collins glass. Add club soda.

Sazerac

As the official cocktail of Louisiana, the Sazerac has a long and fabled history in the city of New Orleans. The Sazerac has a very specific construction. Peychaud's bitters were used in the first renditions of the cocktail in the 1800s and should still be used today.

1 sugar cube
3 dashes Peychaud's bitters
2 ounces rye whiskey
¼ teaspoon absinthe
1 strip lemon peel

Place an old fashioned glass into freezer to chill. Add sugar cube to cocktail shaker. Dash bitters onto cube. Muddle cube to dissolve the sugar in the bitters. Add rye whiskey. Stir. Add 5 ice cubes. Stir 30 seconds. Remove glass from freezer. Add absinthe to it. Swirl to coat the inside of the glass with the absinthe. Strain whiskey mixture into glass. Express essential oils from lemon peel into cocktail by twisting the peel above the surface of the liquid, then rub the lemon peel around the rim of the glass and discard.

Old Fashioned

One of the most quintessential cocktails, the Old Fashioned, when made correctly, has an amazing balance between sweet, bitter, fragrant, and earthy components.

 1 sugar cube

 3 dashes Angostura bitters

 2 ounces Kentucky bourbon

 1 large ice cube

 1 strip orange peel

 1 Luxardo Maraschino cherry

Add sugar cube to an old fashioned glass. Dash bitters onto cube. Add ½ teaspoon water. Muddle cube to dissolve the sugar in the bitters. Add bourbon. Add large ice cube. Stir 30 seconds. Express essential oils from orange peel by twisting above cocktail, then rub the orange peel around the rim of the glass and drop into glass. Garnish with cherry.

Highball

Highball is a class of cocktail comprised of three components: a liquor base, a carbonated beverage, and ice. Think 7 and 7, gin and tonic, or even rum and coke. If you generically order a highball, you leave some interpretation to the bartender, but it will typically default to some type of whiskey and club soda.

> **2 ounces scotch whisky, chilled in freezer**
> **6–8 ice cubes**
> **4 ounces club soda, well chilled**

Add scotch to a chilled highball glass. Add ice cubes. Gently pour in club soda. Stir one or two times, very gently.

"Highballs?" asked the head waiter. "Yes, highballs," agreed Gatsby.

Classic Manhattan

Invented in the Manhattan Club in the late 1800s, the Manhattan is a classic whose recipe needs no modification. This is why it has remained virtually unchanged for the past two hundred years. Using rye whiskey will give it a spicier flavor profile.

3 ounces bourbon or rye whiskey

1 ounce red vermouth

3 dashes Angostura bitters

1 Luxardo Maraschino cherry

Place a martini glass in the freezer to chill. Add bourbon or rye whiskey, red vermouth, and bitters to a cocktail shaker. Add 8–10 ice cubes. Stir vigorously with cocktail spoon for 30 seconds. Remove glass from freezer. Strain cocktail into glass. Add the cherry.

Classic Martini

Shaken or stirred is a question associated with martinis. In general, with all cocktails, those produced with only spirits should be stirred. Those produced with additional ingredients, such as fruit juices, should be shaken.

- 3 ounces gin
- 1 ounce dry vermouth
- 3 cocktail olives

Place a martini glass in the freezer to chill. Add gin and vermouth to a cocktail shaker. Add 8–10 ice cubes. Stir vigorously with cocktail spoon for 30 seconds. Remove glass from freezer. Strain cocktail into glass. Thread olives onto a cocktail pick and add them to the glass.

Mint Julep

When Gatsby, Daisy, Nick, Tom, and Jordan rented a hotel room at The Plaza for an afternoon, the weather was stifling but the conversation was even more heated. It was unfortunate that they never got around to adding Tom's bootleg whiskey to the glasses of mint they summoned from room service. This was the Prohibition way of attaining a mint julep.

12 mint leaves

2 teaspoons superfine sugar

3 ounces bourbon

8 ice cubes

1 mint sprig

Add mint leaves and sugar to a chilled rocks glass. Muddle briefly, allowing the sugar to bruise the mint leaves without tearing them. Leave in glass. Stir in bourbon until sugar is dissolved. Add ice cubes. Stir 5 seconds. Garnish with mint sprig.

Bee's Knees

Popular during Prohibition, this cocktail is said to have been created by a bartender at the Ritz Hotel in Paris in the 1920s. It is a gin sour that uses honey instead of sugar.

1 ounce freshly-squeezed lemon juice

½ ounce honey

3 ounces gin

1 strip lemon peel

Place a champagne coupe in freezer to chill. Add lemon juice and honey to a cocktail shaker. Stir to dissolve honey. Add gin. Continue stirring to make sure honey is completely dissolved. Fill shaker with 8–10 ice cubes. Shake vigorously for 10 seconds. Strain into chilled glass. Rub the lemon peel around the rim of the glass and drop into the glass.

The late afternoon sky bloomed in the window for a moment like the blue honey of the Mediterranean.

French 75 Champagne Cocktail

This cocktail, although named after a French artillery unit from World War I, may or may not have been created before 1922. It is comprised of three highly-touted ingredients from the Gatsby story however: gin, champagne, and lemon.

½ ounce freshly-squeezed lemon juice

1 teaspoon superfine sugar

1½ ounces gin

to top French champagne, chilled

1 strip lemon peel

Place a champagne glass in freezer to chill. Add lemon juice and sugar to a cocktail shaker. Stir to dissolve sugar. Add gin. Add 8–10 ice cubes. Shake vigorously for 10 seconds. Strain into chilled champagne glass. Top with champagne. Rub the lemon peel around the rim of the glass and drop into glass.

FIVE FABULOUS ROARING TWENTIES PARTIES

SUMPTUOUS SELF CARE—
PREP AHEAD SO YOU CAN BE A GUEST.
NOT JUST A HOST

Sometimes we get so wrapped up in the excitement, creativity, and joy of party planning and entertaining our guests, we forget to take care of ourselves. Consider yourself the biggest VIP guest at your party, and make sure your every need is taken of.

If you feel like it, take advantage of a technique that sports champions and successful party planners use. Visualize your victory, from start to finish. Rehearse exactly how the entire event will unfold in your imagination. Do it step-by-step, careful not to skim over anything. Walk through the whole thing in your mind's eye, seeing yourself sharing a most wonderful, low-stress, enjoyable time with your friends. As you picture and see the details, take notes. Envision yourself the day after, feeling tired but jubilant at your entertaining success. Do this several times as the party approaches to see what details you can add and potential disasters you can avoid.

Here are some more handy-dandy helpful hints:

- Plan to have fun and enjoy yourself at every stage of your party, from advance prep to finish.

- Limit tasks once the party gets rolling.

- Select a start and end time for your event and have it on the invitation.

- Make a list of what you'd like to have added by others. That way when someone asks what they can bring, you have an answer ready for them.

- Ask someone if they can be your designated last-minute shopper. Send a quick text if you need more ice or an essential ingredient that a friend can pick up easily on their way.

- Determine the layout of your party materials and decorations in advance. What goes where? Which plates, glasses, napkins, etc.?
- Have fun making your costume the bee's knees! Pick out what you are going to wear ahead of time.
- Choose your music and movies if you want to include them. Make sure you test your technology in advance. Sound checks and test runs are very helpful and stress-reducing.
- If your friends ask if they can help, say yes! They can come early and help decorate or bring food. People love to feel included.
- Create a menu you can accomplish in stages.
- Choose dishes that seem reasonable and possible. You don't need to make every item on the chef's menu. You can mix and match and add your own favorites and specialties.
- Do what works best for you.

- Begin preparing food the day before or even prior to that. Take advantage of the "Party Prepping Plans of Action."
- Remember, most tasks take longer than you think they will. Add plenty of time buffers to your timeline.
- Make sure clean-up, leftovers, compost, trash, and recycle are included in the mix.
- Limit the number of last-minute things you need to do.
- Clean your house early the week of the party. Save minor touch-ups for the day of the event.
- Get professional help for before, after, and during the party itself, if possible, especially for larger events.
- Do as much as you can, as soon as you can, the day of. Take a break. Maybe even have a sip of wine to congratulate yourself.
- Have almost everything done once the party gets rolling. Relax and throw yourself into the swing of the fun!
- Set aside the day after the party for party wrap up and clean up, with help if possible. Relax and revel in your success!

When your fabulous Roaring '20s party is all said and done, what will remain is the fond memory of the joy you brought to others and to yourself. When you look at photos taken or costume pieces hanging about as memorabilia, smile an inner smile and give yourself a warm congratulatory pat on the back. Know that you have contributed something wonderful to making the world a better place. Think of all the lives you've touched. Think of all the fun that was had. Remember the tantalizing tastes you and your guest have loved and enjoyed. You've spread happiness and fun. Well done, old sport!

LADIES'
LUNCHEON
PARTY

Tomato Bisque, Chicken à la King, Jellied Beet Bouillon with Whipped Cream, Pickled Carrots, Mary Ann Cake

The Menu

Prepping Plan of Action

Up to Seven Days Prior

Make and freeze Tutti Frutti Water Ice
Pickle Carrots

Two Days Prior

Make Tomato Bisque to completion
Make mushrooms for Mushroom Toast
Make Jellied Beet Bouillon
Scrape and add Tutti Frutti Water Ice
  to glasses/dishes, freeze

One Day Prior

Make toasts and mayonnaise for
  Mushroom Toast
Make Date Rye Bread
Score Jellied Beet Bouillon (Cut into
  ¾-inch cubes)
Make Chicken à la King
Prep peas for Chicken à la King
Make Mary Ann Cake and unmold,
  refrigerate

Afternoon of Event

Slice Date Rye Bread
Make Ginger Cream for Jellied
  Beet Bouillon
Dice apples and celery for Jellied
  Beet Bouillon
Arrange tomatoes onto plates
  for Endive Salad
Prep remaining ingredients for Endive
  Salad
Remove Mary Ann Cake from
  refrigerator

Prior to Service

Assemble Mushroom Toasts
Assemble Jellied Beet Bouillon
Heat Chicken à la King
Heat Tomato Bisque
Add marmalade to Mary Ann Cake

Time of Service

Toast Date Rye Bread
Garnish Chicken à la King with peas
Assemble and plate-up Endive Salad

Tomato Bisque

Soups, especially bisques and bouillons, were an obligatory course at ladies' luncheons, and were served as a small introductory dish to the meal. Cream was a common component in soups, either blended in to make a bisque, or whipped and served as a dollop atop a bouillon. In the summer, soups would have a lighter consistency. As blenders were not common, soups would only be strained, so they would have had a more textured consistency. In this recipe, we use a blender to achieve a more velvety mouthfeel.

MAKES 1 QUART. SERVES 8 AS AN INTRODUCTORY COURSE.

2 tablespoons olive oil

½ cup yellow onion, finely chopped

½ cup celery, chopped to ¼-inch

¼ cup carrot, grated, peeled

1½ teaspoons paprika

⅓ cup sherry wine

4 cups ripe red tomatoes, diced

2 cloves garlic, sliced

½ teaspoon kosher salt

⅜ teaspoon ground black pepper

1 cup vegetable stock

⅓ cup heavy cream

Add oil to stock pot over medium heat. Add onions, celery, and carrots. Cook, stirring occasionally, for ten minutes. Add paprika. Sauté 10 seconds. Add sherry followed by tomatoes, garlic, salt, and pepper. Bring to simmer. Cook at light simmer for 3 minutes. Add vegetable stock. Again, bring to light simmer. Cook at light simmer for 7 minutes. Stir in cream. Transfer to blender with vented lid. Blend until smooth. Strain through fine mesh colander. Add additional salt and/or pepper if desired.

Mushroom Toast

A toast of some sort was also a part of the standard repertoire of dishes served at luncheons, most often topped with a seafood spread and occasionally with other cooked items such as mushrooms. Mushroom toasts were often made from canned mushrooms. In this recipe, we cook fresh mushrooms and serve them in a typical 1920s style, nicely arranged atop a toast with a flavored mayonnaise spread.

For the Mushrooms

MAKES ABOUT 1 CUP

 2 tablespoons olive oil
 1 pound cremini mushrooms, washed, stemmed, thinly sliced
 2 tablespoons shallots, finely diced
 2 cloves garlic, minced
 Kosher salt to taste
 Ground black pepper to taste
 Pinch ground nutmeg
 1 tablespoon sherry vinegar
 1 teaspoon fresh thyme, chopped

Add oil to large sauté pan over high heat. Add mushrooms, then shallots, and garlic. Add salt, pepper, and nutmeg. Sauté until all liquid in pan has evaporated. Add sherry vinegar and thyme. Again, sauté until liquid has evaporated. Transfer mushrooms to a dish to cool. Refrigerate until needed.

For the Toasts

MAKES 8 TOASTS

⅓ cup mayonnaise

1 teaspoon lemon juice

½ teaspoon lemon zest

Pinch kosher salt

8 thin slices whole wheat sandwich bread

as needed canola oil spray

8 sprigs fresh dill

Preheat oven to 275°F/135°C. Mix mayonnaise, lemon juice, lemon zest, and salt in small mixing bowl. Refrigerate until needed. Use a 3½-inch round cutter to cut 8 circles from the bread. In the absence of a ring cutter, you can cut square or triangular shapes from the bread. Spray both sides of the bread with canola oil spray. Bake on cookie sheet until toasted but not crispy, about 15 minutes. Remove from oven. When cool, spread with lemon mayonnaise. Top with the mushrooms, which may be arranged in a circular pattern or just piled on. Garnish with dill sprigs.

Date Rye Bread

Daintiness was a prevailing attribute of the dishes served at a ladies' luncheon, except where the bread was concerned. Whole grain and hearty breads and rolls were a part of the everyday workings of most kitchens. And in New York in the summer, it was never difficult to find a warm place for the bread to rise.

MAKES 1 LOAF

2½ cups bread flour

1¼ cups dark rye flour

2¼ teaspoons active dry yeast

1 cup whole milk

1 tablespoon unsalted butter

1 teaspoon kosher salt

2 tablespoons molasses

1 cup dates, chopped

Combine bread flour, rye flour, and yeast in medium mixing bowl. Combine milk, butter, salt, and molasses in microwaveable container. Microwave on high for 1 minute or until 125°F/52°C. Stir to melt butter. Stir into flour mixture. Cover bowl with plastic wrap, then kitchen towel, and set in warm place for 1 hour. Turn out onto floured surface and add dates. Knead for 1 minute or until dates are well incorporated, adding bread flour as needed, only to prevent sticking. Place dough into greased loaf pan. Cover with plastic wrap and kitchen towel. Set in warm place for 1 hour. Preheat oven to 350°F/180°C. Bake bread 45 minutes. Remove from pan and let cool on wire rack.

Pickled Carrots

It was a common practice to have small dishes of hors d'oeuvres on the table for the guests to snack on in-between courses, and other small dishes for the guests to enjoy as accompaniments to the meal. These pickled baby carrots serve both purposes. They can be eaten alone or enjoyed together with the main course of Chicken à la King. The crispiness and bright acidity are a great balance to the creamy chicken dish.

3 quarts water

3½ teaspoons kosher salt, divided

1 pound peeled baby carrots

1½ cupscider vinegar

¾ cup granulated sugar

1 tablespoon pickling spice

1½ teaspoons turmeric

½ teaspoon ground black pepper

Bring water and kosher salt to boil over medium high heat. Add carrots. Cook until barely tender. Time will vary depending on size, but approximately 4–5 minutes. Saving 2 cups of the poaching water, transfer carrots to a container of cold water to stop cooking. Clean the pot and place the saved 2 cups of water back into the pot over medium heat. Add remaining ingredients. Bring to a boil. Drain cold water from carrots. Pour the hot liquid over the carrots. Let cool to room temperature. Cover and refrigerate. Will last 14 days in the refrigerator.

Jellied Beet Bouillon with Ginger Cream

Jellied Beet Bouillon is the epitome of daintiness. A flavorful purple-tinted broth is served as fragile little wobbly cubes accompanied by bites of crispy apple and celery and a dollop of fluffy cream, all in a delicate glass coupe.

SERVES 8

For the Jellied Beet Bouillon

- 1 pound large red beets
- 2¼ cups vegetable stock, divided
- ½ yellow onion, peeled, chopped
- 1-inch piecefresh ginger, peeled, sliced
- Pinch cayenne pepper
- ½ teaspoon ground black pepper
- ¾ teaspoon kosher salt
- 1 tablespoon lemon juice
- ¾ teaspoon pickling spice
- 3½ teaspoons unflavored gelatin powder

Trim, peel, and roughly chop beets. Add to blender with 1¾ cups of the vegetable stock, onion, ginger, cayenne, black pepper, salt, and lemon juice. Blend until beets are finely chopped. Transfer mixture to sauce pot over medium high heat. Add pickling spice. Bring to a very low simmer. Cook 20 minutes at barely a simmer. Strain through

4 layers of cheesecloth, squeezing out as much liquid as possible. Measure 1½ cups. Bloom gelatin in remaining ½ cup vegetable stock for 5 minutes. Whisk into hot beet liquid. Pour into a very lightly oiled 8 x 8-inch casserole dish. Refrigerate at least 5 hours or overnight. Score into ¾-inch cubes.

For the Ginger Cream and Presentation

- 1 cup green apple, diced
- 1 cup celery, diced
- 1 teaspoon lemon juice
- 2 tablespoons heavy whipping cream
- ½ teaspoon honey
- Pinch ground black pepper
- ½ teaspoon lemon zest
- 1 teaspoon fresh ginger, grated
- 2 tablespoons mayonnaise

Mix apple, celery, and lemon juice in small mixing bowl. Divide mixture among 8 small glasses or dishes. To the mixing bowl add cream, honey, pepper, lemon zest, and ginger. Whip mixture to soft peaks. Gently stir in mayonnaise. Place a small spoonful of the cream over the apple mixture. Top with jellied beet bouillon cubes followed by another spoonful of cream. Serve chilled.

Chicken à la King

This dish was in its heyday during the 1920s. Although commonly viewed as an American creation, the French sounding "à la" in the name made it seem like a more formal offering. It was very popular at dinners, lunches, and large events like banquets and weddings. When made with high-quality, fresh ingredients, Chicken à la King is quite delicious. Recipes for Tuna Fish à la King appeared at the time as well, using canned tuna. In this recipe, we use just enough flour and cream to give it a silky texture.

MAKES 2 QUARTS

2 pounds chicken thighs, skin-on, bone-in

½ teaspoon kosher salt

1 teaspoonground black pepper

1 tablespoon olive oil

2 onions, peeled, chopped (divided in half)

16 cloves garlic, divided

¼ cup unsalted butter

1 pound cremini mushrooms, washed, stemmed, quartered

⅓ cup all-purpose flour

2 cups celery, chopped

¼ cup heavy cream

Tabasco® sauce to taste

½ cup pimientos, diced

½ cup green peas, cooked

Pat chicken dry with paper towels. Season with salt and black pepper. Add olive oil to stock pot over medium high heat. Brown chicken all over. Add half of the chopped onions and 12 cloves of garlic. Add 5 cups water. Bring to boil. Reduce to simmer. Cover. Cook at low simmer for 45 minutes. Remove chicken to a platter.

Strain the liquid. Skim fat from liquid. You will have about 1 quart stock. Set aside until needed. When chicken is cool enough to handle, remove and discard the skin and bones, and pull apart the meat into pieces. Refrigerate meat until needed. Return the pot to medium high heat. Add butter. When melted, add mushrooms and onions. Season with additional salt and pepper if desired. Chop the remaining 4 cloves of garlic and add. Continue sautéing until mushrooms are fully cooked. Stir in the flour, then the celery. Stir in ½ cup stock. Stir in, scraping the bottom of the pot. Add remaining stock. Fold in reserved chicken meat. Bring to boil, stirring occasionally. Stir in heavy cream. Add additional salt, pepper and Tabasco® if desired. Stir in pimientos. Divide into serving dishes. Garnish with green peas.

Orange Endive Salad

Here is a simply refreshing salad with just enough fancy from the endive. Salads were served after the main dish, as a digestif and refreshing segue to dessert.

MAKES 8 SALADS

- 2 large ripe red tomatoes
- 6 ounces Belgian endive (2 or 3 heads)
- 2 oranges
- 2 tablespoons shallots, minced
- ¼ cup mint leaves, sliced
- 2 tablespoons sherry vinegar
- ¼ cup olive oil
- ½ teaspoon kosher salt
- ¼ teaspoonground black pepper

Slice the tomatoes into halves then crosswise ⅛-inch thick to form semi-circles. Arrange on serving plates in a flower petal pattern. Slice Belgian endives, starting at the tips, crosswise into ¼-inch wide slices. Use a sharp knife to cut the tops and bottoms from the oranges then remove the remaining peel. Cut the oranges into ½-inch pieces, avoiding the center pith. Add orange, endive, and remaining ingredients to mixing bowl. Toss gently to coat. Divide the mixture among the serving plates, arranging it in the center of the tomato slices. Sprinkle with additional ground black pepper. Drizzle any remaining juices in the bowl over the salads.

Tutti Frutti Water Ice

Water ices were another obligatory component to a formal lunch service. They were served prior to dessert. In less affluent households where electric freezers were not yet commonplace, the water ice would be frozen by means of purchased ice and rock salt set into a box, otherwise known as the ice box.

SERVES 16 AS A PRE-DESSERT COURSE
OR 8 AS A STAND-ALONE DESSERT

6 bags mint tea

2 cups water

¾ pound yellow peaches (about 2 large)

½ cup sugar

1 cup freshly-squeezed orange juice

½ cup freshly-squeezed lemon juice

8 mint sprigs

Place tea bags and water in a small sauce pot over medium heat. Bring to a simmer. Turn off heat. Let sit 2 minutes. Meanwhile peel and de-seed peaches. Roughly chop and add to blender. Strain the mint water into the blender. Add sugar, orange juice, and lemon juice. Puree until smooth. Pour into a 9 x 13-inch casserole dish. Place in freezer. Also place your serving dishes or glasses in the freezer. Once frozen, remove dish from freezer and let the ice barely start to thaw. Use a spoon to scrape the surface of the ice into a slushy texture. This works well by scraping with a bit of force in both directions. Transfer the slush to the frozen dishes and place in the freezer until serving. Garnish with mint sprigs.

Mary Ann Cake

A Mary Ann cake refers to the shape of the cake when baked in a Mary Ann-style cake pan, which creates a tall sided cake with a depression in the center that can be filled with fruits, creams, jams, chocolate, or anything the baker desires. As the Mary Ann pan lends itself well to dainty sponge cake and fruits, it would have been a natural choice for a ladies' luncheon.

SERVES 8

4 large egg yolks

¼ cup granulated sugar, divided

1 pinch kosher salt

½ teaspoon ground cardamom

1 teaspoon vanilla extract

1 tablespoon water

½ cup potato starch

4 large egg whites

4 teaspoons cocoa powder

Canola oil spray, as needed

½ cup orange marmalade or other thick jam

Spray an 8- or 9-inch nonstick Mary Ann cake pan. Refrigerate until needed. In absence of a Mary Ann pan, use a 9-inch round cake pan. Preheat oven to 325°F/160°C. Beat egg yolks and half of the sugar in mixing bowl until thick, ribbony, and light yellow. Beat in salt, cardamom, and vanilla. Stir in water. Sift potato starch over yolk mixture. Fold in gently but thoroughly.

In a separate mixing bowl, with clean beaters, whip egg whites until foamy. Add other half of sugar. Continue beating to stiff peaks. Add whites to yolk mixture. Fold in gently but thoroughly. Transfer half of the mixture back to the bowl the egg whites were in. Sift cocoa powder over the top. Fold in thoroughly. Add this dark batter back to the bowl of the light batter. Give it a few stirs to swirl the two batters.

Pour into the prepared pan. Bake 25 minutes or until cake rebounds to the touch when pressed in the center. Transfer to wire rack to cool. Unmold cake. Spread marmalade or jam in the center indentation. Best served at room temperature.

AFTERNOON
TEA

Five-Course Sandwiches, Russian Rosettes, Lower East Side Fermented Pickles, Goldenrod Muffins

The Menu

Prepping Plan of Action

Five Days Prior

Purchase ring cutters for Five-Course Sandwich

Make Lower East Side Fermented Pickles

Two Days Prior

Cook beets for Russian Rosettes

Make French dressing for Russian Rosettes

Boil eggs for Russian Rosettes

Make Harlequin Conserve

Make Lemon Sponge Cake

Make Goldenrod Muffins

Make Chocolate Syrup for Egg Creams

One Day Prior

Slice pineapple for Five-Course Sandwich

Dice pimientos for Five-Course Sandwich

Make Sardine Mixture for Five-Course Sandwich

Make Walnut Mixture for Five-Course Sandwich

Make Lemon Butter for Five-Course Sandwich

Peel eggs, prep yolks and whites for Russian Rosettes

Slice beets and gherkins for Russian Rosettes

Make dressing for Waldorf Salad

Make Ginger Ale Fruit Salad

Glaze Goldenrod Muffins

(CONTINUES)

Afternoon of Event

Remove Lemon Butter from refrigerator to soften for Five-Course Sandwich

Remove cream cheese from refrigerator to soften for Five-Course Sandwich

Dice strawberries for Five-Course Sandwich

Prep ham, watercress, and cucumber for Five-Course Sandwich

Assemble Russian Rosettes

Prep and measure apples with lemon juice, celery, grapes, raisins, and walnuts for Waldorf Salad

Slice pickles

Unmold Ginger Ale Fruit Salad

Prior to Service

Assemble Five-Course Sandwiches

Assemble Waldorf Salads

Time of Service

Assemble Egg Creams immediately before serving

Five-Course Sandwich

The sandwiches Fitzgerald refers to in the book may have been Five-Course Sandwiches—a novel idea at the time and certainly a supper in themselves. A five-course supper to be exact. The concept is to make a pyramid of open-faced sandwiches, graduating in size, and stacked on top of each other. The smallest one on top is the canapé, followed by the fish course, salad course, meat course, and finally dessert. You can also make these sandwiches as individuals.

MAKES 8 SANDWICHES

- **5 ring cutters of graduating sizes between 1 inch and 3.5 inches** (can be purchased as a set online or in baking goods stores)
- **8 fancy, long sandwich picks**
- **8 pumpernickel bread, thinly sliced**
- **8 rectangular white sandwich bread, thinly sliced**
- **8 rectangular whole wheat sandwich bread, thin slices**

For the Sandwich Fillings

- **½ cup cream cheese, softened**
- **8 slices fresh pineapple, cut ⅛-inch thick**
- **⅓ cup strawberries, diced**
- **½ cup pimientos, diced, well drained**
- **8 ounces smoked sandwich ham**
- **1 small bunch watercress**
- **1 small seedless cucumber**

(CONTINUES)

For the Sardine Mixture

1 3.75-ounce tin sardines,
  boneless, skinless, drained
2 tablespoons celery, minced
2 tablespoons mayonnaise
1 teaspoon Dijon mustard
2 teaspoons lemon juice
Pinch of black pepper

For the Walnut Mixture

¼ cup walnuts, finely chopped
1 teaspoon olive oil
1 tablespoon parsley, finely minced

For the Lemon Butter

¼ pound unsalted butter, room temperature
1 lemon, zested

Prepare the Breads

Cut 8 circles of pumpernickel using the largest ring cutter. Cut 8
circles of white bread with the smallest cutter, and 8 more with
the middle-sized cutter. Cut 8 circles of wheat bread with the two
remaining sizes of cutters. We will call the bread circles layers 1, 2, 3,
4, and 5, with 1 being the largest circle and five the smallest. Spread
cream cheese onto layer 1. In small mixing bowl, mix the softened
butter with the lemon zest. Spread onto layers 2, 3, and 5. Layer 4
will stay empty.

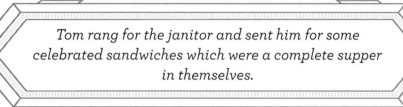

Tom rang for the janitor and sent him for some celebrated sandwiches which were a complete supper in themselves.

Build the Layers

Layer 1: Use a small ring cutter to punch out the middle core of the pineapple slices. Then use the same size cutter that was used to cut the bread to cut the pineapple the same size as the bread. Place pineapple slices on top of the bread and fill the center hole with diced strawberries.

Layer 2: Spread the buttered bread with pimientos. Use the same size cutter you used to cut the bread to cut ham into slices the same shape as the bread. Lay any trimmings of the ham down first, then top with the round cut-out slices.

Layer 3: Pick watercress leaves and cover the entire surface of the buttered bread with them. Slice cucumbers crosswise as thin as possible and arrange them in a shingled pattern atop the watercress. Use about three slices per sandwich.

Layer 4: Combine sardines, celery, mayonnaise, mustard, and lemon juice in small mixing bowl. Mash with a fork to create a consistency similar to tuna salad. Season with black pepper. Spread evenly onto the bread.

Layer 5: Mix together walnuts, parsley, and olive oil and place atop the bread in a thick even layer.

You can now stack the layers on top of each other to create the Five-Course Sandwiches. Layer 1 will be on the bottom, followed by layer 2, and so on. Thread a sandwich pick down the center of each stack.

Russian Rosettes

*Flowers play a prominent symbolic role in **The Great Gatsby**. They were also a common feature at the dining table in the 1920s. Fresh flowers were placed in vases, flower designs were hand painted onto china or etched into glass, and foods were given flowery designs for presentation, such as these Russian Rosettes.*

SERVES 8

For the Rosettes

1 pound extra-large red beets (about 2 beets)

¼ cup French dressing

16 small gherkins

2 hard-boiled eggs, separated into yolks and whites

2 tablespoons mayonnaise

1 teaspoon lemon juice

Kosher salt to taste

Ground black pepper to taste

For the French Dressing

Makes 3 cups

½ cup red wine vinegar

2 teaspoons kosher salt

1 teaspoon ground black pepper

¼ cup Dijon mustard

2 teaspoons ground paprika

1 tablespoon Worcestershire sauce

¼ cup catsup

1½ cups grapeseed oil

1 tablespoon dried basil

To Make the Dressing

Add vinegar, salt, pepper, mustard, paprika, Worcestershire, and catsup to blender. With motor running on medium speed, drizzle in oil in a slow steady stream. Turn off motor. Add dried basil. Pulse just to mix in basil. Keeps up to 2 weeks in the refrigerator.

For Perfect Hard-Boiled Eggs

Place eggs in sauce pot. Cover with cold water by 2 inches. Place over medium heat. Heat until water is as hot as it can get without starting to boil. Maintain at this heat for 5 minutes. Turn off heat. Let sit 10 minutes. Pour off water. Fill pot with cold water to cool eggs. Peel eggs and cut in half. Separate whites and yolks.

To Make the Rosettes

Place beets in a stock pot. Cover with water by 1 inch. Place over high heat. When water comes to a simmer, turn down heat to maintain a light simmer. Cook 30 minutes. Drain off the water.

Fill pot with cold water. Let beets cool to room temperature. Trim top and bottom from beets then peel off the remaining skin. Refrigerate until cold.

Slice beets crosswise into ⅛-inch thick uniform slices. You should have about 16 slices. Lay the slices on a platter. Brush beet slices lightly with French dressing. If gherkins are longer than ¾-inch, trim them down to ¾-inch. Slice each gherkin lengthwise into 5 thin slices. Arrange 5 slices on each beet in a spoke pattern. Use a fork to mash the egg yolks to a smooth paste. Add the mayonnaise, lemon juice, and pinch of salt. Mix until smooth. Spoon a dollop of egg yolk mixture onto the center of each beet. Finely dice the egg white and sprinkle onto the beets. Sprinkle black pepper over the whole platter.

Waldorf Salad

This dish was created prior to the turn of the century at the famous Waldorf-Astoria Hotel in New York City. By the 1920s, the salad was still in vogue. New fanciful versions of the recipe and ways to present it were being developed, such as serving the salad in hollowed out apple cups. The original recipe consisted solely of apples, celery, and mayonnaise, but in the time of Gatsby it would have been more like this elegant rendition.

For the Dressing

MAKES 1 CUP

> 1 raw egg yolk
>
> 1 hard-boiled egg yolk (see Russian Rosettes)
>
> 1 teaspoon onion powder
>
> 1 tablespoon granulated sugar
>
> 1 tablespoon red wine vinegar
>
> 1 tablespoon lemon juice
>
> 1 teaspoon kosher salt
>
> ⅛ teaspoon cayenne pepper
>
> ¼ teaspoon mustard powder
>
> ¾ cup olive oil

Add all ingredients except olive oil to a blender. Turn motor on low speed. Drizzle in olive oil in slow steady stream with the motor running, increasing motor speed as necessary. In absence of a blender, do the same process using a mixing bowl and a whisk.

For the Salad

SERVES 8

- 3 cups apple, skin on, diced to ¼-inch
- 1 tablespoon lemon juice
- 3 cups celery, diced to ¼-inch
- 2 cups red grapes, halved
- 1 cup raisins
- 1 cup walnuts, chopped
- 16 leaves bibb lettuce
- Ground black pepper to taste

Add apples and lemon juice to large mixing bowl. Toss to coat. Add celery, grapes, raisins, and walnuts to apples. Toss again. Just before serving, add 1 cup of the dressing. Lay 2 leaves of bibb lettuce onto each plate. Top with Waldorf Salad. Season with black pepper over the top.

Lower East Side Fermented Pickles

Barrels of naturally pickled cucumbers filled the sidewalks of Lower East Side Manhattan in the 1920s. Pickles of all kinds were commonly served as accompaniments to multi-course menus. To get more serious about pickling, you may want to acquire a pickling jar with a fermentation lid, which allows gasses to escape. In this more modest method, we use a jar with a loosely fitted lid. Cucumbers are actually one of the trickier vegetables to pickle. You may use this same recipe to naturally pickle cauliflower, peeled beets, carrots, or string beans, too. If it's your first time pickling, you may want to try making one-third of the recipe.

MAKES ABOUT 3 POUNDS

3 pounds pickling cucumbers (about 1 dozen)

2 ounces fresh dill

10 cups non-chlorinated water

¼ cup + 1 teaspoon kosher salt

15 cloves garlic, peeled

1 teaspoon celery seeds

2 teaspoons yellow mustard seeds

1½ teaspoons pickling spice

¾ teaspoon red chili flakes

5 bay leaves

Wash cucumbers in cold water. In a large jar or container that has a lid that can be loosely placed, add sprigs of dill followed by a layer of cucumbers, and so on, until the dill and cucumbers are layered in the jar. Place 2 cups water, salt, garlic, and all remaining seasonings in sauce pot over medium heat. Bring to a simmer then turn off heat, stirring to dissolve the salt. Remove from stove and cool to room temperature.

Add this to the remaining 8 cups water, then pour into the container of cucumbers. Cucumbers should be fully submerged and liquid should be at least 2 inches below the top of the container. Weigh down the cucumbers so that they stay submerged. Using a water filled plastic zip-lock bag is a good way to weigh them down. Put a loose-fitting lid on the container. Place container inside of another pan in case of spill-over. Place in a dark, cool place such as a kitchen cabinet or garage.

After 72 hours check for signs of fermentation such as bubbling and cloudiness. Once you see bubbles, transfer the container to the refrigerator or ferment one or two more days for a tangier pickle, before transferring to refrigerator. Enjoy within 3 weeks.

The pickles can be sliced and served in a small dish or dishes in the center of the table or may be served directly on the plates containing the Five-Course sandwiches.

Harlequin Conserve

The word harlequin is often used to describe a medley of varied colors. This conserve is composed of yellow, orange, green, and blue-colored fruits. The finished product should be a composition of the different fruits but not a blending of them, hence the instructions to stir gently and infrequently during the cooking process. This would be served as an hors d'oeuvre to be snacked on in-between courses.

MAKES ABOUT 5 CUPS

1 cup pineapple, diced

½ cup granulated sugar

¾ teaspoon anise seeds

1 pound yellow peaches, pitted, diced

1 large orange, peeled, diced

25 seedless green grapes, halved lengthwise (about 1 cup)

6 ounces blueberries (about 1 cup)

Add pineapple, sugar, and anise seeds to sauce pot over medium heat. Cook, stirring often until sugar dissolves and reduces to a thick syrup, about 5 minutes. Add peaches and oranges. Return to boil. Cook until the juices reduce and become syrupy again, about 8 minutes. Stir as little and as gently as possibly during this phase to prevent breaking up the fruit. Gently fold in the grapes. Cook until the juices reduce and become syrupy again, about 5 more minutes. Turn off the heat. Gently fold in the blueberries. Let mixture cool in the pot to room temperature. Transfer to glass or plastic containers. Refrigerate until cold. Cover. Will keep 7 days refrigerated.

Ginger Ale Fruit Salad

To be chic, trendy, and with-it in the 1920s kitchen, you had to serve your salads molded into fancy shapes and designs. Gelatin was the key component that facilitated this. Flavoring the gelatin adequately may not have been a commonly attained result by modern standards. This version is a classic Ginger Ale Fruit Salad recipe, tailored to today's palate by increasing the ratio of goodies to gelatin and by switching the ginger ale for the higher quality and more intense flavor of ginger beer.

SERVES 4

- 1 tablespoon unflavored gelatin
- 2 tablespoons cold water
- 2 tablespoons granulated sugar
- 1 cup ginger beer
- ¼ cup lemon juice
- ¾ cup apples, diced, skin on
- ¾ cup oranges, sliced, no peel, no pith
- ¾ cup seedless grapes, halved lengthwise
- ¾ cup banana, diced
- ½ cup walnuts, chopped
- ¼ cup candied ginger, diced or sliced
- Vegetable oil, as needed
- 8 leaves bibb lettuce

(CONTINUES)

Soak gelatin in cold water for 5 minutes. Add sugar. Bring some additional water to boil, measure ¼ cup, and stir into the bloomed gelatin. Stir in ginger beer. Refrigerate. In large mixing bowl, combine lemon juice, apples, oranges, grapes, bananas, walnuts, and candied ginger. Toss to coat fruit with lemon juice. When ginger beer mixture begins to show signs of gelling, add to the fruit mixture. Add to a 48-ounce jello mold that has been lightly coated with vegetable oil. You may also divide into four 12-ounce molds or glasses. To unmold, run the tip of a paring knife around the perimeter of the jello to loosen. Dip the molds in warm water for 10–15 seconds. Turn over onto a serving platter or individual plates lined with lettuce leaves.

Lemon Sponge Cake

When Nick invited Daisy over for tea, he had twelve lemon cakes at the ready from the delicatessen shop. He and Gatsby scrutinized the cakes together, prior to Daisy's arrival. This moment of great anticipation accompanied by the last-minute checking of details is relatable to anyone hosting guests, and even more so if awaiting the arrival of a long-lost love. This lemon sponge cake, with its pudding-like bottom layer and spongey top, will certainly impress.

MAKES ONE 9-INCH CAKE

- ⅓ **cup unsalted butter, room temperature**
- ⅔ **cup granulated sugar, divided**
- **2 large egg yolks**
- ⅓ **cup lemon juice**
- **1 tablespoon lemon zest**
- ¼ **cup all-purpose flour**
- **1 cup whole milk**
- **2 large egg whites**

Preheat oven to 350°F/180°C. In mixing bowl, beat butter and half of the sugar until well mixed. Beat in egg yolks, lemon juice, lemon zest, and salt. Mix in flour and milk.

(CONTINUES)

In separate bowl with clean beaters, beat egg whites until foamy. Add remaining ⅓ cup sugar. Beat until stiff peaks. Fold egg whites into the mixture. Pour into a 9-inch oven proof serving dish (such as glass or ceramic pie dish). Place the dish inside of another larger pan. Pour hot water into the larger pan, halfway up the sides of the pie dish. This is easier to do if the pans are inside the oven when pouring in the water. Bake 35 minutes or until top is golden and springs back when touched, but bottom is still custardy. Remove from oven. Let pie dish cool to room temperature on a wire rack before refrigerating. You can serve it warm from the oven or at room temperature.

Goldenrod Muffins

Tea time is the only meal service where more than one dessert is not only welcome, but expected. This recipe is a revival of a cake which was popular during the time of Gatsby, but was lost, like Daisy, to the passage of time. It was baked in triangular-shaped cake pans called goldenrod pans, and a variation of this recipe was called Waldorf Triangles. This cake has a golden color from the egg yolks and a wonderfully pocked texture with a flavor that is not overly sweet. Except for their shape, this recipe is an almost unaltered version of the one found in the 1921 cookbook, American Cookery.

MAKES 6 MUFFINS

For the Muffins

   6 egg yolks
   ½ cup granulated sugar
   2 tablespoons orange juice
   1 tablespoon orange zest
   Pinch kosher salt
   ½ cup all-purpose flour
   1 teaspoon baking powder

Preheat oven to 325°F/160°C. Add egg yolks and sugar to mixing bowl. Beat until thickened and a light-yellow color. Stir in orange juice, orange zest, and salt. Sift flour and baking powder over the yolk mixture. Mix in. Transfer to greased muffin tins, filling ⅔ full. Bake 13–15 minutes. Cool on wire rack. Remove from pan when still warm.

(CONTINUES)

For the Glaze

    2 teaspoons orange juice
    ⅓ cup powdered sugar

Mix together and drizzle over the muffins after they are cooked.

Egg Cream

The refreshing effervescent chocolatey drink called an egg cream, which does not contain eggs nor cream, was a mainstay of the infamous prolific candy store scene of 1920s New York City. There are various opinions on what the authentic construction of the recipe is, but most everyone agrees that it contains three ingredients: chocolate syrup, milk, and soda water. Here, we make a thick homemade chocolate syrup so that it is not too sweet, extra chocolatey, and it stays on the bottom of the glass when pouring in the milk. For a party setting, you can fill the glasses with the chocolate and the milk then refrigerate until needed, and add the soda water at the moment of service.

Chocolate Syrup

MAKES 10 OUNCES, ENOUGH FOR 10 EGG CREAMS

- 1 cup unsweetened cocoa powder
- ⅔ cup granulated sugar
- ½ teaspoonkosher salt
- 1 cup water
- 1 tablespoon vanilla extract

Add cocoa powder, sugar, and salt to medium sauce pan. Whisk until the cocoa powder has no lumps. Use the whisk to stir in the water and vanilla extract. Whisk until smooth. Place over medium heat. Cook, stirring with the whisk constantly until it barely starts

(CONTINUES)

to simmer. Remove from heat. Transfer to a sealable container. Refrigerate until chilled. Cover. Will keep refrigerated for 7 days.

To Make Each Egg Cream

> **2 tablespoons chocolate syrup**
> **¼ cup whole milk**
> **1 cup chilled soda water**

Add chocolate to a 12-ounce glass. Pour milk over chocolate. Place tall spoon in the glass. Right before serving, add the soda water to the glass and hand to your guest. Have them stir it to create a nice head of foam and drink right away!

SIT-DOWN
DINNER

Cream of Celery Soup, Sliced Beef in Mustard Sauce, Pineapple Upside-Down Cake

The Menu

Prepping Plan of Action

Two Days Prior

Make Cream of Celery Soup to
   completion
Make Cocktail Sauce for Crab
   Cocktail-Stuffed Alligator Pears
Cook pineapple and syrup for
   Pineapple Upside-Down Cake
Roast the beef then refrigerate beef
   and stock for Sliced Beef with
   Mustard Sauce
Make French dressing for June Salad

One Day Prior

Trim the fat and slice the beef roast
   for Sliced Beef with Mustard Sauce
Make the Mustard Sauce
Arrange sliced beef, potatoes, and
   carrots on oven-proof serving
   platter for Sliced Beef with
   Mustard Sauce
Prep and blanch vegetables for
   June Salad
Make and bake Pineapple Upside-
   Down Cake, refrigerate

Afternoon of Event

Mix Crab Cocktail
Mix and plate-up June Salad,
   refrigerate
Unmold Pineapple Upside-Down
   Cake

Prior to Service

Heat Celery Soup
Prep avocados and stuff with Crab
   Cocktail
Heat Mustard Sauce on stovetop
Heat beef in oven for Sliced Beef
   with Mustard Sauce
Remove June Salad from refrigerator
Remove Pineapple Upside-Down
   Cake from refrigerator

Cream of Celery Soup

Celery was a big deal during the time of Gatsby. There were serving dishes which were decorated etched glass vases or oblong ceramic platters dedicated solely to the service of celery sticks. Celery played the star or a supporting role in many dishes of the time. This soup would be served for lunch or dinner as part of a multi-course menu.

MAKES 6 CUPS

2 tablespoon sunsalted butter

1 cup yellow onion, chopped

4 cups celery stalks, roughly chopped

1½ teaspoons kosher salt

¾ teaspoons ground white pepper

Pinch ground nutmeg

2 bay leaves

¾ teaspoon celery seeds

1 quart vegetable or chicken stock

¼ pound gold potatoes, peeled, chopped

1 cup heavy cream

1 cup curly parsley leaves, tightly packed

1 lemon, zested

Melt butter in stock pot over medium heat. Add onion and celery. Cook 3 minutes, stirring often. Add salt, white pepper, nutmeg, bay leaves, and celery seeds. Cook 2 minutes, stirring often. Add vegetable stock and potatoes. Bring to a simmer. Simmer gently for 20 minutes. Remove and discard bay leaves. Turn off heat. Stir in cream. Working in small batches, add the soup, parsley leaves, and lemon zest to a blender. Puree until smooth. Strain through colander. Add additional salt and/or pepper if desired.

Crab Cocktail-Stuffed Alligator Pear

In the 1920s, avocados were commonly referred to as Alligator Pears, since the term avocado had just been introduced less than ten years prior. Seafood cocktails were wildly popular, especially in the muggy summer months. The refreshing, cold temperature of the dish along with a bit of spice functioned to help cool bodies down.

SERVES 8

For the Cocktail Sauce

- ⅓ cup catsup
- ¼ cup lemon juice
- ¾ teaspoon Tabasco® sauce
- ½ teaspoon kosher salt
- ¼ teaspoon celery seeds
- ¼ teaspoon ground black pepper
- ¼ teaspoon lemon zest
- 1½ teaspoons Worcestershire sauce
- 1½ teaspoons prepared horseradish

Mix all ingredients together in small mixing bowl. Refrigerate until needed.

For the Crab Cocktail-Stuffed Alligator Pears

½ pound lump blue crab meat

6 tablespoons red onion, finely diced

2 tablespoons capers, chopped

4 avocados

1 lemon, juiced

pinch kosher salt

8 sprigs parsley, for garnish

Add crab meat, onion, capers, and cocktail sauce to mixing bowl. Mix gently. Halve the avocados lengthwise. Remove pits. Peel avocados. Slice enough off the bottom of each avocado half to create a flat surface to prevent toppling. Brush entire surface of avocados with lemon juice. Sprinkle lightly with salt. Fill avocados with crab mixture. Garnish with parsley sprigs.

Sliced Beef in Mustard Sauce

This is not only a great dish to prepare in two steps, but the result is actually better that way (see Chef's Tip below). Mustard was another well-loved and commonly-used condiment of the time. This dish makes a wonderful homestyle Sunday supper.

SERVES 8 AS PART OF A 5-COURSE DINNER
OR SERVES 6 ON ITS OWN

1 3-pound/1.36kg beef chuck roast

2 teaspoons kosher salt

2 teaspoons finely ground black pepper

2 tablespoons olive oil

1 large yellow onion, chopped

1 cup red wine

1 cup beef stock

12 cloves garlic, peeled

12 sprigs fresh thyme

6 sprigs fresh marjoram

1 pound baby potatoes, halved

½ pound carrots, peeled, cut into 2-inch pieces

½ cup Dijon mustard

1½ teaspoons ground turmeric

Preheat oven to 300°F/150°C. Season chuck roast with kosher salt and black pepper. Place large cast iron skillet or Dutch oven on stovetop over medium high heat. Choose a pot with room enough to hold the roast, vegetables, and stock. Add olive oil. When very hot, add seasoned chuck roast and brown thoroughly on all sides. Add onions to the pan around the meat. Let onions cook 1 minute. Add red wine, beef stock, garlic, thyme, and marjoram. Cover with tight fitting lid or aluminum foil. Place in oven for 2 hours.

Add potatoes and carrots to the meat. Re-cover. Cook additional hour. Remove meat, carrots, and potatoes from the liquid.

For the Mustard Sauce

Strain the liquid from the roasting pan into a small sauce pot. Skim fat from the top. You will have about 1½ cups liquid. If less, add beef stock; if more, reduce to 1½ cups. Place sauce pot of liquid over medium heat. Whisk in Dijon mustard and turmeric. Simmer gently for 5 minutes.

Slice beef thinly, removing any fat. Fan out slices on oven-proof serving platter. Arrange potatoes and carrots around meat. Reheat in oven. Ladle some mustard sauce over meat and serve remaining sauce on the side.

Chef's Tip

Follow instructions, up until straining the stock, one or two days ahead. Refrigerate meat and the strained liquid overnight. This makes it easier to cut the meat into beautiful thin slices, and to remove the fat from the stock, which will now be congealed on top.

June Salad

In summer months, cold salads were served to help relieve diners from the heat. French dressing was a popular and in vogue condiment and used to dress just about any single vegetable or combination of vegetables imaginable.

SERVES 8

1 pound thin green asparagus stalks

¾ pound green string beans

½ pound carrots, yellow or orange

1 cup fresh green peas

1 cup red cabbage, shaved

6 ounces red beets, cooked or pickled, peeled, diced

¾ cup French dressing

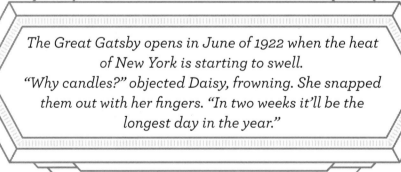

The Great Gatsby opens in June of 1922 when the heat of New York is starting to swell.
"Why candles?" objected Daisy, frowning. She snapped them out with her fingers. "In two weeks it'll be the longest day in the year."

Trim and discard tough bottom portion of asparagus stalks. Chop remaining stalks into ¼-inch pieces, reserving 1 inch of the tips. Trim string beans. Chop into ¼-inch pieces. Peel and trim carrots. Dice into ¼-inch squares. Bring 6 cups of lightly salted water to boil over high heat. Have an ice bath on hand. Add chopped string beans to water. Cook until tender. Remove from the water and transfer to ice bath. Repeat with asparagus stalks and tips, then diced carrots, and then peas. Drain all vegetables from ice bath and pat dry with paper towels. Transfer to large mixing bowl. Add cabbage and beets.

Add French dressing. Toss to coat. Season with salt and pepper if desired. Arrange on a serving platter.

Pineapple Upside-Down Cake

This is one of the most quintessential, even clichéd, 1920s dishes. The distribution of canned foods at the time brought new, exotic, and exciting ingredients to home kitchens. Pineapple from Hawaii, though canned, was a trendy and elegant new ingredient for many cooks. Pineapple Upside-Down Cake was a great way to showcase the prized fruit to dinner guests. To make this recipe gluten-free, use ½ cup potato starch instead of all-purpose flour.

SERVES 8 FAMILY-STYLE

For the Pineapple and Pan

- 1 small fresh pineapple
- 1 cup granulated sugar
- 1 cup water
- 8 candied cherries, pitted, stemmed

Trim and peel pineapple. Cut crosswise into ¼-inch thick slices; you will need 6 slices. Use small cookie cutter or melon baller to punch out the core of each slice. Add sugar and water to large sauté pan over medium high heat. Bring to simmer. Working in batches, place the pineapple slices in the syrup. Return to a simmer. Cook 3 minutes, turning over once. Transfer to plastic wrap-lined cookie sheet to reserve until needed. Continue cooking the syrup until it caramelizes to a golden brown. Immediately pour into 9 × 13-inch metal baking pan, tilting pan to allow syrup to cover the bottom. You need to do this quickly, as sugar will thicken and harden rapidly as it cools. When cool, line bottom of pan with pineapple slices.

Place cherries in the spaces that are not covered by pineapple. Set aside briefly while preparing the batter.

For the Batter

- 6 large eggs, separated
- ⅛ teaspoon ground allspice
- 4 tablespoons granulated sugar (divided in half)
- ⅓ cup dark rum
- ½ cup cake flour, sifted

Preheat oven to 350°F/180°C. In large mixing bowl, beat egg yolks, allspice, and half the sugar until thick and ribbony. Stir in rum and flour. Set aside. In separate bowl, beat egg whites to soft peaks. Add remaining sugar. Beat until stiff peaks. Fold into yolks using rubber spatula. Pour batter evenly into prepared pan.

Bake 30 minutes or until skewer inserted in center of cake comes out clean. Remove from oven.

Let stand 15 minutes. Insert paring knife between cake and edge of pan to loosen all the way around. Place large serving platter on top of pan. Carefully and quickly invert cake onto serving platter.

If cake is not loose in the pan, or if you baked it ahead and refrigerated, place pan over medium flame for 15–30 seconds or until caramel loosens and cake moves freely in the pan, then invert.

THE SPEAKEASY MENU

Oysters à L'ancienne

The Menu

Prepping Plan of Action

Three or More Days Prior

Make Nesselrode Pudding, freeze

Two Days Prior

Make Meatballs and tomato sauce to completion
Make seasoned flour mixture for Fried Chicken
Make Turkey Hash to completion
Prepare bacon and butter for Oysters à L'ancienne

One Day Prior

Measure all ingredients for Welsh Rarebit sauce
Brine chicken for Fried Chicken
Make and form Potato Cod Cakes

Afternoon of Event

Make toasts for Welsh Rarebit
Unmold Nesselrode Pudding
Open oysters for Oysters à L'ancienne

Prior to Service

Reheat Meatballs
Cook cheese sauce for Welsh Rarebit
Fry Chicken
Reheat Turkey Hash
Fry Potato Cod Cakes
Place Oysters in baking dish, top with butter and bacon

Time of Service

Assemble Welsh Rarebits
Fry eggs for Turkey Hash if desired
Bake Oysters

Meatballs

Many of the thousands of speakeasy establishments in New York City were operated by Italian immigrants. Typically, the husband would act as barman, and the wife would run the kitchen. For many patrons, this was their first experience with authentic Italian cooking, and meatballs were a very popular item to be offered up.

MAKES 12 MEATBALLS

For the Meatballs

⅔ cup herbed bread crumbs

⅔ cup water

1 large egg

½ cup Pecorino Romano cheese, grated

¼ cup parsley, chopped

3 cloves garlic, finely chopped

1 teaspoon kosher salt

½ teaspoon ground black pepper

1 pound ground beef chuck

2 tablespoons olive oil

Add bread crumbs to large mixing bowl. Stir in water. Add the egg, cheese, parsley, garlic, salt, and pepper. Mix to blend. Add the beef. Mix quickly just until evenly blended. Divide into 12 portions. Shape into balls. Transfer to oiled baking sheet. Place into refrigerator to firm up while making the sauce.

For the Sauce

¼ cup thin-cut smoked bacon, chopped (2 strips)

2 tablespoons olive oil

½ cup onion, finely chopped

2 cloves garlic, chopped

3¼ cups tomatoes, strained (one 750ml box)

½ teaspoon dried oregano

⅛ teaspoon red chili flakes

to taste kosher salt

Chop the bacon. Add oil and bacon to sauce pot over medium heat. Stir frequently until bacon browns. Add onion. Cook, stirring frequently until onion browns lightly. Stir in garlic, then strained tomatoes, oregano, chili flakes, and salt. Bring to simmer. Simmer 5 minutes. Turn off heat. Leave on stove top.

To Finish

Bake meatballs in preheated 400°F/200°C oven for 10 minutes. Transfer to tomato sauce. Return tomato sauce to medium heat. Bring to simmer. Simmer meatballs for 10 minutes, turning once during cooking and occasionally spooning tomato sauce atop meatballs. Meatballs need to reach a minimum internal temperature of 165°F/74°C before serving.

Welsh Rarebit

Welsh Rarebit was popular for informal and formal gatherings, and a great way to make use of leftover breads, especially hearty whole grain breads. Welsh white cheddar gives the dish the most authenticity, but yellow cheddar was also commonly used. Some recipes from the 1920s did not call for ale or beer since Prohibition was in effect. This dish can be made using milk in place of both the beer and cream. Some original recipes added raw egg for creaminess, but using a blender allows us to omit that step. For best results, grate the cheese as opposed to purchasing pre-grated cheese.

If you serve a fried egg atop a Welsh Rarebit the name changes to Buck Rarebit. This dish pairs wonderfully with a pint of ale.

MAKES 2½ CUPS OF SAUCE

- 2 tablespoons unsalted butter
- 2 tablespoons all-purpose flour
- 8 ounces beer, preferably stout, IPA, or amber ale
- 1 tablespoonWorcestershire sauce
- ¾ cup heavy cream
- 1 teaspoon ground black pepper
- Pinch of cayenne (plus more for garnish)
- ½ teaspoon dried mustard
- Pinch of ground nutmeg
- 8 ounces sharp cheddar cheese, grated
- 8 slices bread, toasted (pumpernickel, whole grain, or sourdough are best)
- ½ cup scallions, sliced

Add butter to a medium sauce pan over medium heat. As soon as butter melts, stir in flour to make a roux. Continue stirring until roux turns a golden color. Turn off heat. Immediately whisk in beer, mixing until smooth. Stir in Worcestershire sauce, heavy cream, pepper, cayenne, dried mustard, and nutmeg. Bring to a boil. Transfer to blender. Turn to lowest speed. With motor running, sprinkle in cheese. Continue blending until smooth. Return to sauce pan. Set over very low heat to keep warm. To serve, drizzle generously over slices of toast. Sprinkle with scallions and a dash of cayenne.

To Make Ahead

Refrigerate the sauce. Before serving, bring additional ½ cup beer to a simmer in small sauce pot. Add the cold sauce one large spoonful at a time, whisking constantly until it comes up to a simmer. Serve.

Fried Chicken

On the night of the accident, Daisy and Tom sat at the kitchen table with a plate of cold fried chicken. Neither of them touched the chicken. Although they weren't in the mood for eating, if the cooks had used this recipe, they might have been less able to resist!

SERVES 4

Buttermilk Brine the Chicken

    2 cups buttermilk
    1½ teaspoons kosher salt
    1 teaspoon ground black pepper
    2 tablespoons Worcestershire sauce
    4 teaspoons Tabasco® sauce
    2½ pounds chicken thighs and/or legs, bone-in, skin-on

Add buttermilk, salt, pepper, Worcestershire, and Tabasco® to large container. Mix thoroughly. Pat chicken pieces dry with paper towels. Transfer to buttermilk mixture, ensuring they are submerged. Cover. Refrigerate overnight, up to 24 hours.

Bread the Chicken

    1½ cups all-purpose flour
    ⅓ cup cornstarch
    1 teaspoon fine sea salt
    1 teaspoon ground white pepper
    ½ teaspoon cayenne
    ½ teaspoon dried oregano

Mix all ingredients together in a casserole dish. Remove chicken pieces from the buttermilk brine and transfer them to a cookie sheet lined with 2 layers of paper towels. Dip each piece of chicken in the flour mixture, rolling to coat. Leave it in the dish of flour while dipping the other pieces. Once pieces are all coated, discard the paper towels from the cookie sheet and replace them with plastic wrap. Transfer floured chicken pieces to the plastic wrap lined sheet. Let them sit 5 minutes. Re-dip one piece at a time into the flour, gently shake off excess flour, then place back on the cookie sheet.

Fry the Chicken

3 cups frying oil (i.e., canola, vegetable, grapeseed)

Add oil to heavy bottom stock pot or cast-iron pan over medium heat. If you have a thermometer, bring oil to 325°F/160°C. If not, heat until the oil bubbles moderately when chicken is added. Lightly shake excess flour from chicken. Place 3 or 4 pieces of chicken in oil, without crowding the pan. Monitor heat to maintain the oil lightly bubbling. Cook 15–18 minutes, turning over a few times as they cook. Dark meat chicken should reach a minimum internal temperature of 175°F/80°C. Remove to paper towel-lined baking sheet. Let rest 5–10 minutes before serving.

Turkey Hash

At the speakeasy where Nick lunched with Gatsby and Wolfsheim, across the street from the Old Metropole, a succulent hash arrived at the table to accompany their round of highballs. In this recipe, we use turkey bacon to ensure the necessary amount of succulence, along with gold potatoes and pimientos, which were a staple of the 1920s pantry.

SERVES 4

2 tablespoons olive oil

1 cup onion, chopped

2 cups Yukon gold potatoes, ⅜-inch diced, unpeeled

1 tablespoon unsalted butter

8 ounces turkey bacon, cut crosswise into ½ inch pieces

½ cup celery, diced

4 cloves garlic, thinly sliced

⅛ teaspoon cayenne

2 tablespoons sherry vinegar

½ cup pimientos, chopped and well drained

1 tablespoon fresh thyme, chopped

4 large eggs, if desired

Add oil to large non-stick sauté pan over medium high heat. Add onion and potato. Sauté until potatoes and onions are lightly browned, about 5 minutes. Add butter. Continue sautéing to brown further, about 2 minutes. Add turkey bacon, celery, and garlic. Sauté 2 minutes. Add cayenne and cook additional 2 minutes. Add vinegar, pimientos, and thyme. Stir until the pimientos are evenly distributed, then turn off heat. May be served with a fried egg on top if desired.

Potato Cod Cakes

Fried foods that were easy to eat and easy to serve were an effective strategy to boost revenues at the tens of thousands of speakeasies that sprung up in New York City in the early 1920s. This dish is made with cod, but salmon is a great substitute. It is wonderful served with the Orange Endive Salad and may also be accompanied by the cocktail sauce used for the Crab Cocktail-Stuffed Alligator Pear.

SERVES 4

1½ pounds fresh cod fillets, boneless, skinless

to taste kosher salt

to taste ground white pepper

6 tablespoons olive oil (used in 3 different steps)

2 teaspoons thyme, freshly picked

1 pound russet potatoes, peeled

2 tablespoons unsalted butter

½ cup buttermilk

8 cloves garlic, thinly sliced

1 tablespoon onion powder

Pinch grated nutmeg

½ teaspoon baking powder

1 cup all-purpose flour

Preheat oven to 350°F/180°C. Cut cod into 8 pieces. Transfer to casserole dish. Season with salt and pepper. Add 1 tablespoon olive oil and thyme leaves, coating the fish. Cover dish with plastic wrap and then foil. Set aside. Cut potatoes into ½-inch cubes. Transfer to separate casserole dish. Add butter, buttermilk, garlic, onion powder, and nutmeg. Season with salt and pepper. Cover with plastic wrap then foil. Place cod and potatoes in oven. Remove cod after 15 minutes. Bake potatoes additional 30 minutes or until tender.

Transfer potatoes and contents of their dish to large mixing bowl. Mash potatoes until smooth. Break cod up into large flakes, discarding the pan juices. Fold baking powder, 3 tablespoons olive oil, and flaked cod into potatoes. Add additional salt and/or pepper if desired. Form mixture into 8 balls. Dredge in flour, shaking off excess. Press into 3-inch cookie cutter ring to form patties. Add remaining 2 tablespoons olive oil to large nonstick skillet over medium heat. When hot, working in two batches, place patties in skillet. Fry 1 minute on each side or until golden brown. Transfer to lightly-oiled baking sheet. Bake 8 minutes or until hot.

To Make Ahead

After forming the cakes in a cookie cutter, cover and refrigerate up to 2 days. After frying, transfer to lightly-oiled baking sheet and bake at 350°F/180°C until hot in the middle, about 8 minutes.

Oysters à L'ancienne

The French name of this dish translates to Oysters in the Old Style. Various recipes existed, but the thing they all had in common was bacon and baking the oysters. Often lemon juice and butter were also added before baking. In this recipe, we make a flavored butter, use a generous amount of it, and, oh yes—add some bacon too, old sport.

MAKES 2 DOZEN

24 medium sized oysters

8 strips thin-cut smoked bacon

1 tablespoon unsalted butter

¾ cup cremini mushrooms, finely diced, stemmed

⅓ cup green bell pepper, finely diced

¼ cup scallions, white and/or green part, finely sliced

¼ cup pimientos, finely diced, well-drained

2 tablespoons lemon juice

⅜ teaspoon ground black pepper

⅓ cup unsalted butter, softened

1 pound rock salt

Wash whole oysters in cold water. Shuck oysters, discarding top shell. Dip bottom shell, with oyster still attached, in salted ice water, to remove debris. Detach oysters from shells, leaving meat in the shell. Refrigerate until needed. For food safety, it's a good idea to transfer every six oysters into refrigerator, as you shuck them. Cut each strip of bacon crosswise into 3 equal pieces. Place large nonstick sauté pan over medium heat. Add butter. When melted, add 8 pieces bacon. Cook until just starting to brown on edges. Turn over and do the same on the other side, then remove to paper towel-lined plate. The bacon will be semi-cooked.

When all bacon has been processed, add mushrooms and bell peppers to pan with the bacon grease. Sauté just until no longer raw. Transfer to mixing bowl. Cool to room temperature. Stir in scallions, pimientos, lemon juice, pepper, and softened butter. Mix thoroughly. Preheat oven to 400°F/200°C. Place rock salt in large casserole dish or oven-proof skillet. Nestle oysters into salt so that they are lying flat. Spoon a rounded teaspoon of the butter mixture onto each oyster. Top with one slice of the semi-cooked bacon. Bake until hot in the center, 10–12 minutes, depending on size. Oysters need to reach an internal temperature of at least 145°F/63°C. Let cool 5 minutes before serving.

Nesselrode Ice Pudding

Ice pudding was as gourmet a dessert as you could get in 1800s England. New versions were invented for and named after queens and others of nobility. They were served in elaborate molded shapes on platters made of ice. This recipe was created a hundred years prior to Gatsby by a French chef in honor of the Russian diplomat Karl Von Nesselrode. In the 1920s, puddings were associated with the elegance of Victorian England, and iced desserts were a status symbol. Iced pudding brought these two ideas together. Many households still used Victorian tableware they may have inherited, received as a wedding gift, or simply purchased. During Prohibition, the quality of liquor suffered, so using alcohol in a dessert like this would mask the imperfections. Soaking the currants in the brandy keeps them from freezing too hard. If you can't find currants, use raisins. In the absence of candied ginger, you may omit it.

SERVES 8

- ⅔ cup dried currants
- ¼ cup candied ginger, finely diced
- ¼ cup brandy
- 10 ounces unsweetened canned chestnut puree (may be purchased online)
- 3 large egg yolks
- ¼ cup granulated sugar
- 1 teaspoon vanilla extract
- 2 cups heavy cream (divided into 1½ cups and ½ cup)

This is a molded frozen confection. You have different options of molds. Metal rings lined with plastic strips or parchment paper, a lightly oiled Bundt pan, individual sized metal molds, or silicon molds. In the absence of molds, you can also freeze in glasses or dishes. Total volume of this recipe is about 48 ounces.

Add currants, candied ginger, and brandy to small container. Cover. Let soak at least 1 hour. Crumble chestnut puree into blender. Add yolks, sugar, and vanilla to blender. Add 1½ cups heavy cream to sauce pan over medium heat. Bring to barely a simmer. Turn off heat.

With blender motor running, add hot cream in a steady stream, blending until smooth. Transfer to large mixing bowl.

Clean sauce pan. Add 2 inches water to it. Place back on stove over medium high heat. Set bowl of chestnut mixture atop sauce pan of boiling water. Cook, whisking constantly until mixture visibly thickens and coats the back of a spoon. Remove from heat. Let sit on counter top to cool for 15 minutes, stirring often. Refrigerate until completely chilled, stirring every 5 minutes. Stir in the currant brandy mixture. Whip remaining ½ cup heavy cream to stiff peaks. Fold into chestnut mixture. Transfer to your selected mold(s). Cover. Freeze.

To unmold from a metal pan, dip the mold very quickly (as little as 2 seconds) in hot water. Invert mold onto a plate. You may need to use the tip of a knife to coax the dessert out of the mold.

THE GLORIOUS
GALA

Salmon and Caviar Checkerboard, Spiced Baked Ham, Relish Canapés, Strawberry Bavarian Cream, Harlequin Chicken Salad

The Menu

Prepping Plan of Action

Two Days Prior

Make toasts and boil eggs for Daisy
    Canapés

Boil eggs for Deviled Eggs

Prepare Stuffed Pimientos, except
    for baking them

Make blue cheese mixture for
    Stuffed Celery

Prepare Harlequin Chicken Salad up
    to when you refrigerate the chicken

One Day Prior

Make Anchovy Butter for Relish
    Canapés, if using

Make white and yellow mixtures for
    Daisy Canapés

Make sardine mixture for Daisy
    Canapés

Prepare Pastry Pigs except for
    baking them

Prep celery sticks for Stuffed Celery

Peel and slice eggs for Deviled Eggs

Make yellow (yolk) mixture for
    Deviled Eggs

Prepare Savory Cheese Ball

Prepare Spiced Baked Ham, except
    for baking it

Continue Harlequin Chicken Salad
    until refrigerating the mold

Prepare Strawberry Bavarian until
    refrigerating the mold

(CONTINUES)

Afternoon of Event

Bake Spiced Baked Ham

Assemble Relish Canapés

Assemble Daisy Canapés

Prepare Salmon and Caviar
  Checkerboard

Remove blue cheese mixture
  from refrigerator to soften for
  Stuffed Celery

Assemble Deviled Eggs

Unmold Harlequin Chicken Salad

Unmold Strawberry Bavarian

Prior to Service

Bake Pastry Pigs

Assemble Stuffed Celery

Garnish Harlequin Chicken Salad
  with watercress

Time of Service

Bake Stuffed Pimientos

Daisy Canapés and Classic Martini

Daisy Canapés

*There is no denying the significance of daisies in **The Great Gatsby**. This recipe is inspired by a similar recipe we discovered in the 1922 cookbook, **Hospitality: Recipes and Entertainment Hints for All Occasions**, published the same year Gatsby and Daisy reunite. We show you how to make a daisy design on a round cut of bread, but you can also acquire a daisy-shaped cookie cutter and use daisy-shaped pieces of bread.*

MAKES 12 CANAPÉS

For the Toast

12 slices sandwich bread, thinly sliced
Canola oil spray, as needed

Preheat oven to 300°F/150°C. Using a daisy-shaped or round ring cutter, cut a 3-inch circle or daisy shape from each slice of bread. Spray both sides with canola oil. Place on baking sheet. Bake approximately 15 minutes or until lightly toasted. Cool.

For the Eggs

4 large eggs

Place eggs in sauce pot. Cover with cold water by 2 inches. Place over medium heat. Heat until water is as hot as it can get without starting to boil. Maintain at this heat for 5 minutes. Turn off heat. Let sit 10 minutes. Pour off water. Fill pot with cold water to cool eggs. Peel cooled eggs. Cut eggs in half. Separate yolks from whites.

(CONTINUES)

For the White Mixture

   4 hard-boiled egg whites

   1 tablespoon lemon juice

   1 tablespoon mayonnaise

   ¼ teaspoon kosher salt

   ⅛ teaspoon ground white pepper

Add all ingredients to food processor. Blend until as smooth as possible. Transfer to small pastry bag with small tip.

For the Yellow Mixture

   4 hard-boiled egg yolks

   1 teaspoon mayonnaise

   ⅛ teaspoon turmeric

   ¼ teaspoon Tabasco® sauce

   ⅛ teaspoon kosher salt

   Pinch ground white pepper

   ½ teaspoon olive oil

Add egg yolks to small mixing bowl. Mash as smooth as possible with tines of a fork. Add remaining ingredients. Mash until smooth again. Roll ½ teaspoon of mixture into a ball then flatten to make a circle.

For the Sardine Mixture

1 3.75-ounce can sardines, boneless, skinless, drained

2 tablespoons celery, minced

2 tablespoons mayonnaise

1 teaspoon Dijon mustard

2 teaspoons lemon juice

Pinch black pepper

In small mixing bowl, mash ingredients together to form a sardine salad. Spread 1 tablespoon mixture onto each toast circle. Pipe 7 to 9 half-inch circles of egg white mixture around the perimeter of the toast, just barely touching each other. Use small spoon to pull the center of each circle towards the center of the toast. The goal is to form a flower petal shape. Place a yolk circle in the center of the whites, to look like a daisy flower.

Relish Canapés

Relish platters are great to serve at a large gathering, to be snacked on at the guests' leisure during the course of the evening. Relishes during Gatsby's time were typically a combination of raw and pickled or marinated vegetables served with one or more dips. In this version, we show you how to serve the relish as individual skewers in a fancy presentation worthy of a gala setting.

MAKES 16 CANAPÉS

1 small pineapple, whole

as needed canola oil spray

optional edible flowers, organically-grown with short stems

16 small radishes, trimmed

16 cornichons

16 cocktail olives

16 cocktail onions

16 cherry tomatoes

16 5-inch long bamboo or wooden skewers

Cut bottom off of pineapple so that it can stand upright. Use scissors to trim the ends of all of the leaves. Spray leaves with canola oil so they have a shiny appearance. If using, stick flowers into the spaces between the leaves for presentation. Thread each skewer with one radish, cornichon, olive, onion, and tomato. Stick skewers into pineapple, all around, to resemble a porcupine.

Place on a platter with flowers around the base of the pineapple, if desired. Serve anchovy butter in a bowl or ramekins for guests to dip if they'd like.

Optional Anchovy Butter

    1-ounce can anchovies, drained

    1 teaspoon lemon zest

    ⅓ cup unsalted butter, softened

Place anchovies in small mixing bowl. Use tines of fork to mash into a paste. Stir in lemon zest. Add butter, mashing and stirring to make a paste. Transfer to serving dish or ramekins.

Salmon and Caviar Checkerboard

Patterns in composition were a strategic way to enhance the presentation of food. By making two simple canapés and composing them into a checkerboard pattern, we can elevate the fancy factor. You can use whatever level of caviar you wish. The more inexpensive caviars may be saltier, so taste it and adjust the quantity used accordingly.

SERVES 8 AS A CANAPÉ

> 1 tablespoon capers, drained
>
> ½ cup unsalted butter, softened
>
> 1 teaspoon lemon zest
>
> 4 slices whole wheat sandwich bread, thinly sliced
>
> 4 slices white sandwich bread, thinly sliced
>
> 4 ounces black caviar
>
> 6 ounces smoked salmon, sliced
>
> 16 chive sticks, 1-inch long

Set aside 16 capers. Add softened butter and remaining capers to mixing bowl. Using tines of a fork, mash and stir until well blended and spreadable. Spread caper butter evenly onto the 8 slices of bread, keeping in mind that you will be squaring off the edges of the bread. Spread caviar onto the slices of buttered white bread. Lay smoked salmon in an even layer over the slices of buttered wheat bread.

Using a sharp knife, square off each slice of bread so that you end up with 1 large square that is covered entirely with either the salmon or the caviar (the cook gets to snack on the trimmings!). Cut each large square into 4 equally-sized smaller squares. Arrange in 2 checkerboard patterns on separate platters. Top each salmon square with 1 reserved caper. Top each caviar square with 1 chive stick.

Stuffed Pimientos

Pimientos figured very prominently in the 1920s kitchen. Pimiento (also called pimento) refers to a variety of bright red peppers, typically of Spanish origin, that are roasted and jarred with a bit of an acidic flavor from their marinade. The piquillo pepper, a perfect size for stuffing as an appetizer, is one type of pimiento. They are commonly found in the preserved vegetable section of grocery aisles. To make this recipe vegan, remove bacon from the recipe and add 1 additional tablespoon olive oil.

SERVES 8

4 tablespoons olive oil, divided

4 ounces or 4 slices thin-cut smoked bacon, diced

¾ cup red onion, finely diced

2½ cups stemmed cremini mushrooms finely chopped

1 cup green apple, finely diced

½ cup dates, chopped

1 teaspoon fresh thyme, chopped

¼ teaspoon ground black pepper

⅜ teaspoon kosher salt

2 teaspoons sherry vinegar

2 tablespoons herbed dry bread crumbs

14-ounce jar piquillo peppers, whole roasted (about 16)

Add 2 tablespoons olive oil and bacon to large nonstick skillet over medium heat. Cook, stirring until bacon browns. Add onions, mushrooms, and apples. Sauté until mushrooms are cooked and any liquid has evaporated. Stir in dates, thyme, pepper, and salt. Add sherry vinegar. Turn off heat. Fold in bread crumbs. Allow to cool. Preheat oven to 350°F/180°C. Carefully stuff peppers with mushroom mixture. Place in single layer in baking dish. Drizzle with remaining 2 tablespoons olive oil. Bake 10 minutes.

Blue Cheese-Stuffed Celery

In the cookbook, Mrs. Allen on Cooking, Menus, Service, published in New York in 1924, Mrs. Ida Allen gives a recipe for celery ribs stuffed with Roquefort and cream cheese. She suggests removing the celery strings, but by using the more tender inner ribs we skip that procedure. In this recipe, you can use any kind of blue cheese, and we have added a garnish of dried cherries to give a sweet balance to the pungency of the filling.

MAKES 12

   12 4-inch pieces celery ribs, cut from inner medium sized ribs
   ¼ pound blue cheese, crumbled
   ¼ cup cream cheese
   1 teaspoon Worcestershire sauce
   ⅛ teaspoon ground black pepper
   ½ cup dried cherries

Wash and dry celery. Beat blue cheese, cream cheese, Worcestershire, and black pepper together until incorporated but still textured. You can use beaters, food processor, or mash thoroughly with tines of a fork. Fill celery sticks using a spoon or pastry bag. Sprinkle with additional black pepper to taste. Place 3 dried cherries atop the blue cheese, equally spaced.

Deviled Eggs

This is a basic but delicious recipe with an impressive balance between the spice, tang, and creaminess. Garnish with a sprig of dill and sprinkle of cayenne to add even more complexity. You can create variety by using different garnishes such as chives, caviar, or crispy bacon. It's fun at a Gatsby party to make two platters of deviled eggs embellished differently and label them East Eggs and West Eggs.

MAKES 8

4 large eggs

1¼ teaspoons olive oil

2 teaspoons lemon juice

¼ teaspoon Tabasco® sauce

⅛ teaspoon turmeric

⅛ teaspoon kosher salt

Pinch ground white pepper

1½ tablespoons mayonnaise

⅜ teaspoon ground dried mustard

Pinch cayenne pepper

8 large sprigs fresh dill

Place eggs in sauce pot. Cover with cold water by 2 inches. Place over medium heat. Heat until water is as hot as it can get without starting to boil. Maintain at this heat for 5 minutes. Turn off heat. Let sit 10 minutes. Pour off water. Fill pot with cold water to cool eggs.

(CONTINUES)

Peel cooled eggs. Cut in half lengthwise. Remove yolks and transfer them to food processor.

Add olive oil, lemon juice, Tabasco®, turmeric, salt, pepper, mayonnaise, dried mustard, and pinch of cayenne to same food processor. Blend until smooth. Transfer to pastry bag fitted with a small star tip. Pipe yolk mixture into the egg whites. Garnish each with a dash of cayenne and sprig of dill.

Savory Cheese Ball

An easy way to dazzle the crowd. Take some ordinary chèvre goat cheese and dress it up to the nines. We use fine little Zante currants, chopped nuts, a bit of basil, and make it dashing with a dash of black pepper.

SERVES 8

- **11-ounce log Chèvre goat cheese**
- **¼ cup walnuts or pecans, finely chopped**
- **¼ cup dried Zante currants**
- **½ teaspoon dried basil**
- **¼ teaspoon ground black pepper**

Cut log of goat cheese in half. Let soften up enough to be able to roll each into a ball that nicely holds its shape. Mix walnuts or pecans, currants, basil, and pepper in medium mixing bowl. Place 1 ball of goat cheese into the mixture. Roll and press cheese ball into the mixture to coat. Wrap in plastic wrap. Repeat with the other ball of cheese. Refrigerate to firm up the cheese. Remove from refrigerator 15 minutes before serving.

Pastry Pigs

The pastry pigs mentioned here are presumed to be what are now commonly referred to as Pigs in a Blanket. Using a high-quality link sausage gives them enough gourmet for a gala. If you like to keep things on the spicy side, try a nice andouille.

MAKES 16

   8 links pre-cooked sausages (3- to 4-ounces each)
   1 sheet puff pastry, approximately 10 × 10-inches
   All-purpose flour, as needed
   ½ cup whole grain mustard
   1 large egg, well beaten
   1 tablespoon sesame seeds
   2 teaspoons poppy seeds

Cut sausage links in half crosswise to make 16 pieces. If using frozen puff pastry, transfer to refrigerator until softened enough to roll out. Using a rolling pin and a floured work surface, roll out puff pastry to half its original thickness, keeping the edges as straight as possible. While rolling, dust with flour as necessary to prevent sticking. Trim edges to straighten. Cut into eight rectangles, approximately 2½ inches × 5 inches. Cut rectangles in half diagonally to create 16 right triangles.

On buffet tables, garnished with glistening hors d'oeuvres, spiced baked hams crowded against salads of harlequin designs and pastry pigs and turkeys bewitched to a dark gold.

Lay triangles with pointed ends facing away from you. Spread 1½ teaspoons mustard onto the side of the triangles that are towards you. Place the sausage atop the mustard. Brush the remaining exposed surface of the puff pastry lightly with the beaten egg. Roll tightly from the end closest to you to the tip of the triangle, trying to manipulate the rolling so that the tip of the triangle ends up towards the middle of the roll. Transfer to lightly oiled baking sheets. Brush beaten egg onto remaining exposed surface of the puff pastry. Sprinkle with sesame seeds and poppy seeds. Refrigerate at least 30 minutes to firm up pastry dough, and up to 1 day, if prepared ahead of time. Preheat oven to 400°F/200°C. Bake until crispy and bewitched to a dark gold, about 20–25 minutes.

Spiced Baked Ham

Spiced baked hams crowded the buffets of Gatsby's weekend galas. Gatsby intended to impress, and a large ham sitting nobly on the table, with the sight and scent of its shimmering glaze, was a sure way to attract the guest's attention.

SERVES 8

1 small fresh pineapple

1⅓ cups brown sugar

1 cup water

⅓ cup rye bourbon

½ teaspoon ground allspice

1 teaspoon ground ginger

2 tablespoons dried mustard powder

⅛ teaspoon cayenne

1 6-pound ham roast

9 candied cherries, pitted, stemmed

Soak 40 toothpicks in cold water. Set aside until needed. Trim and peel pineapple. Cut crosswise into seven ¼-inch thick slices. Use a small cookie cutter or melon baller to punch out the core of each slice. Add brown sugar and water to large sauté pan over medium heat. Bring to simmer. Working in batches, place the pineapple slices in the syrup. Return to a simmer. Cook 3 minutes, turning over once. Transfer to plastic wrap-lined cookie sheet to reserve until needed.

Once all pineapple slices are poached, stir the rye bourbon, allspice, ginger, mustard powder, and cayenne into the syrup. Return to medium high heat. Continue simmering until reduced to a glaze consistency, 4–10 minutes. You should have about 1 cup. Set aside and keep warm.

Preheat oven to 300°F/150°C. Place ham, fat side up, on a roasting rack set in a roasting pan. Add ½ inch of water to the roasting pan. Brush ham generously with the glaze. Bake uncovered, 90 minutes, brushing every 20 minutes with additional glaze.

After 90 minutes, remove from the oven and use soaked toothpicks to fasten pineapple slices and cherries to ham. Brush with additional glaze. Raise oven temperature to 375°F/190°C. Bake additional 60 minutes, brushing with glaze every 15 minutes, until ham reaches an internal temperature of 145°F/63°C. If ham over browns during any point of the process, cover with foil until the cooking is finished. Allow to rest 15 minutes before slicing.

Harlequin Chicken Salad

Nick Carraway speaks of salads of harlequin designs at Gatsby's party. During this time, salads did not typically refer to lettuce, rather to compositions of various ingredients bound together with gelatin and molded into fancy presentations. We designed this recipe to replicate a 1920s Chicken Salad, with a few small adjustments to account for modern tastes. We used barely enough gelatin to perform its task, and designed the broth to have a nice intensity of flavor. Harlequin designs were achieved by cutting out diamond shapes of ingredients, such as carrots or truffle paste, and lining the mold with them so that when unmolded the design is presented. We mimic that by using cross slices of different colored carrots to get a similar effect.

MAKES 1 SMALL PLATTER FOR 4–6 PEOPLE

   1 pound chicken thighs, skin-on, bone-in

   1½ teaspoons kosher salt, divided in 2 steps

   ¾ teaspoon ground black pepper, divided in 2 steps

   1 tablespoon olive oil

   1 cup red onion, diced to ¼-inch, divided in 2 steps

   4 cloves garlic, roughly chopped

   1 teaspoon pickling spices

   1 medium yellow carrot, trimmed, peeled

   1 medium orange carrot, trimmed, peeled

   1 tablespoon unflavored gelatin powder

   ¼ cup red bell pepper, diced to ¼-inch

¼ **cup green bell pepper, diced to ¼-inch**

½ **cup celery, diced to ¼-inch**

3 tablespoons fresh lemon juice

½ **teaspoon Tabasco® sauce**

⅓ **cup cornichons, chopped to ¼-inch**

1 bunch watercress, washed

Pat chicken dry with paper towels. Season with ¼ teaspoon kosher salt and ¼ teaspoon ground black pepper. Add olive oil to stock pot over medium high heat. Add chicken, skin side down. Brown chicken all over. Add ½ cup diced red onions, garlic, pickling spice, and 4 cups water. Bring to boil. Reduce to light simmer. Cover tightly. Cook at low simmer for 45 minutes. Remove chicken to a plate. Strain the liquid and place in freezer. When fat has risen to the top, skim fat from liquid. You will have about 3 cups stock. Set aside until needed. When chicken is cool enough to handle, remove and discard the skin and bones, and pull apart the meat into pieces. Chop into approximately ⅜-inch pieces. Refrigerate until needed.

Using a mandolin slicer, slice 12 thin rounds crosswise from the thick end of each carrot. Dice remaining part of carrots into ¼-inch dice, approximately ¾ cup total. Set diced carrots aside. Add sliced carrots and ½ cup chicken stock to small sauce pan over medium heat. Bring to a boil then immediately strain the stock back into the larger amount of stock. Refrigerate the poached carrot slices until needed.

Bloom gelatin in ¼ cup water for 5 minutes. Set aside until needed. Add all of the chicken stock to sauce pot over medium heat. Reduce to approximately 2 cups. Add 1¼ teaspoon kosher salt, ½ teaspoon black pepper, and the diced carrots. Bring to simmer. Cook 2 minutes. Add red and green peppers, celery, and remaining ½ cup red onion. Cook 1 minute. Turn off heat. Stir in bloomed gelatin, lemon juice, Tabasco®, cornichons, and chopped chicken.

(CONTINUES)

Place the poached carrot slices onto the inside surface of a Bundt pan, arranging them in a pattern of alternating colors. They should stick on their own. When the liquid in the chicken mixture starts to become visibly viscous, carefully ladle the mixture into the pan without disturbing the placement of the sliced carrots. Cover. Refrigerate at least 4 hours. To serve, dip pan into a container of hot water for 10–15 seconds. Invert onto serving dish. Place watercress in middle of the ring.

Strawberry Bavarian Cream

Desserts were designed to delight the eye just as much, if not more than, the tongue. The beauty of this recipe lies in its ease of preparation compared to how dramatic it can be in presentation. Have fun using molds of various shapes and designs. Since this has a flowery pink color, flower shaped molds not only work very well here, but also pay tribute to the symbolism of flowers in the book.

SERVES 6–8

- **5 teaspoons unflavored gelatin**
- **½ cup cold water**
- **1 pound fresh strawberries**
- **½ cup granulated sugar**
- **1 cup heavy cream**

This is a molded, refrigerated dessert. You have different options of molds. Metal rings lined with plastic strips or parchment paper, a lightly-oiled Bundt pan, or individual-sized metal molds will all work. Silicon molds are not recommended. In the absence of molds, you can also use glasses or dishes. Total volume of this recipe is about 36 ounces.

Mix gelatin with water. Set aside to bloom. Remove hulls from strawberries. Chop strawberries into ⅜-inch pieces. Add to large sauté pan over medium heat. Add sugar. Cook, stirring gently, just until sugar dissolves and strawberries lose their raw appearance.

(CONTINUES)

Turn off heat. Stir in gelatin to dissolve. Transfer to medium bowl and cool to room temperature. Refrigerate strawberry mixture briefly until it becomes slightly viscous but not set. In the meantime, add heavy cream to different large mixing bowl. Whip to stiff peaks. Fold strawberries into whipped cream, quickly but thoroughly.

Transfer to molds or serving dishes. Refrigerate until set, at least 4 hours. Unmold by dipping mold very briefly into a container of hot water then inverting onto a serving plate.

ROARING
TWENTIES
FASHION

THAT'S ONE HOT TOMATO SHOWING OFF THOSE GAMS!— FASHION IN THE 1920S

Upper class fashion of the times is exquisitely described in *The Great Gatsby*. Here are some quotes from the book: *A chauffeur in a uniform of robin's egg blue. Girls in yellow dresses. Gown of gas blue with lavender beads. Men in white knickerbockers and caramel-colored suits. His gorgeous pink rag of a suit made a bright spot of color against the white steps...*

The fashion world went mad in the '20s—mad with freedom! There was a revolution that shortened women's dresses, simplified style, and never looked back.

This rebellion didn't just come out of nowhere. It was overdue following "the war to end all wars," or as we now refer to it, the brutal, bloody, World War I. It was relief from the end, finally, of the Spanish Flu pandemic that killed over 50 million people worldwide. The transformation was also egged on by positive factors. In the United States, the first women—gasp—actually got the right to vote! The stock market was really taking off and more people participated than ever. The economy was booming.

Finally, it was also a reaction to the controversial temperance movement that got Prohibition passed in 1920 and opened up a whole new industry of speakeasies and rum runners. This created a rich environment for mobsters and new opportunities to freely dress up and unleash the wildest fashion self.

Hot tomatoes (hot women) were showing off their *gams* (legs) all dolled up and ready to party! Getting *zozzled* on *giggle water* standing in a speakeasy was a highly desirable, trendy-yet-edgy activity for newly liberated women of all ages. The fashionable men were wearing pants with sharp creases and cuffed hems above fancy spectator shoes. Men could ask

a buddy to spot them a few *clams* (money), and their gal would be the *bee's knees* (the best).

Hems were up, tight fitting bodices were out, waists were dropped closer to the hips or eliminated altogether. And thank goodness, the old-fashioned personal torture device known as a corset was on its way out.

The new, even boyish styles for women came with an emphasis on flatter chests; some amply endowed women even bound their breasts to appear flatter. Simplified undergarments were adopted in part to allow for easier movement, especially for the new, freer dance moves. Yet, it was still more than that. It was a very deliberate rejection of Victorian-era restrictions in behavior, dress code, and social expectations.

Use of different fabrics added to the rebellion. Gone were lace, velvet, and heavy brocades. Durable, breathable, less expensive cotton usage boomed in the 1920s. Treated (mercerized) cotton, lightweight and sheer cotton voile, and denim-like chambray found great popularity. Wool became fashionable, including the now iconic wool jersey. And rayon, made of processed wood pulp, became popular, replacing for many the more expensive silk. The natural fiber linen was considered even more hygienic and exceedingly enjoyed, particularly in hotter climates.

They were both in white, and their dresses were rippling and fluttering as if they had just been blown back in after a short flight around the house.

Daywear for women consisted of dresses that went up to the knee (but no further), long or three-quarters length sleeves, and a skirt that was straight, pleated, or tiered. This look was topped off by a loose coat of the same fabric or similar and the ubiquitous cloche hat.

Evening wear was a bit more flamboyant with the classic flapper dress that featured a long-fringed hem, also called the Charleston dress, with no waistline but plenty of movement on the dance floor. And good heavens—feathers, feathers, feathers were everywhere! Feather boas topped long, multiple-strands of pearls that were also a must of the day. Jeweled headbands were adorned with feathers sticking straight up.

Dresses and coats all fluttered through the evening with feathers literally flying. It was the flapper look completed with a long cigarette holder and silk stockings held up by garters that could be glimpsed as dancers whirled on the floor.

To reinforce the boyish look, for the first time in history, large numbers of women cut their hair into short styles such as the bob cut, the Marcel wave, and the very masculine Eton crop. Even those who were too timid to take the plunge and cut their hair bound it up so that it appeared shorter.

The sister, Catherine, was a slender, worldly girl of about thirty, with a solid, sticky bob of red hair, and a complexion powdered milky white. Her eyebrows had been plucked and then drawn on again at a more rakish angle...

For women, the look was accentuated with more makeup, including *smokey* eyes, plucked eyebrows, and pouty lips, highlighted with the dark red lipsticks that were all the rage. Painted on in a *Cupid's Bow*, the red lipstick was the most popular makeup trend of the time.

A sportier and freewheeling look was also in fashion for those in Gatsby's high economic circles. Designers were creating looks for both men and women that had a more active look, like tennis or badminton wear, even if you never set a foot on a court. It was all part of the trend towards freer and more relaxed movement, a simplified style that meant less was more.

Still, that didn't mean that simplicity was inexpensive. The chic look of the well-dressed flapper was claimed by some to cost as much as it would to equip a reasonably well-furnished three room flat. And that expense wasn't restricted only to women. Heavily influenced by popular athletic wear, *plus fours*, a baggy-leg pant that narrowed below the knee, topped with a Scottish Fair Isle sweater or V-neck tennis style sweater, became daily casual wear for men. Wide-leg trousers with a sharp crease and cuffs finished off another new look for men, with waist-slimming belts rather than suspenders.

He took out a pile of shirts and began throwing them, one by one, before us, shirts of sheer linen and thick silk and fine flannel, which lost their folds as they fell and covered the table in many-colored disarray. While we admired he brought more and the soft rich heap mounted higher—shirts with stripes and scrolls and plaids in coral and apple-green and lavender and faint orange, with monograms of Indian blue.

Although there were many emerging designers whose names are still recognizable over a hundred years later from Lanvin, to Jean Patou, to Louise Boulanger, no discussion of 1920s fashion would be complete without mention of Coco Chanel. Credited with creating *the modern woman,* Chanel associated with the bohemian elite of Paris and brought a freedom of style to women's clothing, accessories, and even fragrance.

Chanel did indeed fuel the fashion revolution by her endorsement and use of trousers for women, encouraging also the use of costume jewelry, even for those who could afford the real thing. Her introduction of jersey for women's clothing, which until then was only used for men's underwear, was nothing short of a radical innovation. She also literally invented the *little black dress,* an item which still, a hundred years later, no fashionable woman is without. So influential was Coco Chanel, that she is the only clothing designer listed on *Time* Magazine's 100 Most Influential People of the 20th Century.

I hope she'll be a fool—that's the best thing a girl can be in this world, a beautiful little fool.

Ha! *Horse feathers* to that old-fashioned notion! Sit back with your Gin Rickey and flamboyantly toss your feather boa over your shoulder. People and fashion now, and in the 1920s, are *jake* with me!

FOR THE FASHIONISTA—
GATSBY ATTIRE BY PARTY

Ladies' Luncheon—Do Come to Lunch

Luncheons in the 1920s were a somewhat dressy affair and required clothing a bit fancier than normal day dress. Even middle-class women had a
semi-formal dress that they would turn to for a luncheon invitation.

These dresses were adorned with silver or gold metallic threads, creating elaborate embroidered designs on the collar, belt, hems, and sleeves.
Hand-painted designs were also popular and emulated embroidery. Hems
were shorter, though still not above the knee, with dropped waists, and the
jazz-age gals of the time started mixing both print and solid patterns into
the fashions.

As the decade wore on, these dresses became the backdrop for
ever bolder accessories such as larger purses, long shawls, furs, and the
ever-present hat! This way, if you had to get through a dreadfully dull luncheon engagement with your great aunt Agatha, at least you were armored
in the smart attire of the day.

Afternoon Tea—Do Come in for a Cup of Tea

And with that invitation in the 1920s, you knew you were one of the popular crowd. Afternoon tea parties, particularly in the summer, were all the
rage, often including some lawn games like croquet, bocce, or badminton. As a see-and-be-seen event, the attire was certainly more formal than
morning or day wear, but not as fancy as sleeveless evening wear.

> *Mrs. Wilson had changed her costume some time before, and was
> now attired in an elaborate afternoon dress of cream-colored chif-
> fon, which gave out a continual rustle as she swept about the room.
> With the influence of the dress her personality had also undergone
> a change.*

The upper crust of the time often wore white, and you knew they were well-to-do because white was very hard to keep clean. It indicated you had servants to take care of everything. The middle-class tended to stick to colors of dusty rose, blue, green, yellow, or lilac.

Her face, above a spotted dress of dark blue crêpe-de-chine, contained no facet or gleam of beauty, but there was an immediately perceptible vitality about her as if the nerves of her body were continually smouldering.

Women's dresses tended to be lightweight and sheer, made out of everything from silk to linen. Outfits would be finished off with gartered stockings, Mary Jane shoes with a bit of a heel, white cotton gloves, and a straw hat. During the winter, fabrics worn to tea were more appropriate to the season, including light wool and taffeta.

Men also had to wear the appropriate attire for tea, and while more relaxed than ever, there were still fashion rules to be followed. Jay Gatsby wore an afternoon white suit that included a waistcoat and spats. Other men wore striped trousers, a high silk hat, and gray or dove-colored gloves. Together these smartly-dressed men and women would promenade and flirt all through afternoon tea.

Dinner and Evening Gala Party—The Pleasure of Your Company is Requested

Whether you were invited to a home for a sit-down meal, to a mansion for a formal dinner, or to a ballroom for a gala, in the 1920s the more opulent your dress-style the better. For women, the flat-chested, loose-fitting dress remained through the evening, but that's where the resemblance to day dress ended. It was the time of the invention of the cocktail dress and the difference was like day and night.

And I like large parties. They're so intimate. At small parties there isn't any privacy.

Hems were shorter, up to the knee or mid-calf, with beaded, scalloped, embroidered, and/or uneven handkerchief hems, making them each a standout in their own way. The dropped waistline was often gathered or draped for a unique, flowing look. This was also a time that introduced the dramatic low scoop and deep V in the back of the dress, making both front and back an attraction. The one thing that was not worn in good company was the all-fringe, short flapper dress.

The Art Deco movement brought popular geometric shapes and patterns to the dresses. New Egyptian archeological finds and interest in Asian art made decorative pins and accessories in those styles all the rage for evening wear. Dress clips (like pins, but with a clip on the back) were often added to the point of the V neck or in pairs, if the neckline was square. Hats were gone, replaced with shimmering hair decoration that included rhinestones and feathers. And the fabrics! Nothing would do but the richest. Everything from velvet to satin and gold and silver lamé were *de rigueur*.

Gentlemen still wore top hats and tailcoats, but the more casual dinner jacket—what we would call a tuxedo jacket—was introduced at this time. Men also had the option of wearing the more daring pin-striped or solid-colored white suits accented with brightly colored ties in pinks or reds. Couples moving through these fabulous evening events were practically dripping with glamour with every step they took!

Speakeasy Glad Rags—The Password Is...

Once the secret word had been uttered and the club entered, women shrugged off their rich velvet coats and furs and let their inner flapper fly free! This wild, jazz-crazed gal wore a sleeveless dress that's at the knee or—gasp—slightly above. Adorned with heavy beading and rhinestones, the hem was finished off with a long fringe that really moved when the dancing started and kept the gentlemen's eyes on those gams!

Slinging back her bathtub gin, she was lavish and glamorous with a sparkly tiara, long pearl necklaces, golden arm bangles, and a fabulous feathered fan or boa draped around her neck.

The guys accompanying the gals often kept the traditional evening look, perhaps with the more relaxed dinner jacket. Another choice was a

cream-colored dinner jacket. Some men chose to abandon the formal look altogether and adopted striped suits, flashy neckties, Homburg hats, shoe spats, and gold-capped walking sticks. They topped it all off with a racoon fur coat. Quite the dandies, these cool cats loved showing off with and for their flapper dolls. They danced the night away!

> *A phrase began to beat in my ears with a sort of heady excitement: "There are only the pursued, the pursuing, the busy, and the tired."*

FOR MORE CASUAL PARTY FASHION

Easy Ways to '20s Up Your Look

Costumes can be easy and fun! Getting a '20s look doesn't have to send you digging through the vintage clothing stores, unless that's your thing, and then, have at it! Gals, grab a headband, glue gun, and strategically place sparkles and feathers. Guys, pull some argyle socks over your pant legs for knickerbockers and add a sweater vest over a collared shirt. Voilà!

Here are a few ideas for costuming:

- Argyle socks
- Feather boa or feather fan
- Flapper dress
- Fringe
- Fur–faux or antique
- Gloves
- Hats–cloche, fancy, fedora, newsboy, straw
- Headband with sparkles and feathers
- Little black dress
- Long beads or pearls
- Spectator/saddle shoes
- Suit jacket
- Suspenders
- V-neck sweater

Dress Up Your Home for Your Party

The same way that party costumes can be easy and fun, the décor for your home can be too. Hit the antiques stores; yard, garage, or tag sales; thrift stores; or Etsy for just a few featured pieces. Martini glasses, Art Deco anything (repro-ductions work just fine), Lusterware or floral-painted dishes, or really whatever tickles your fancy. Stick stalks of celery in a vase and you'll have a very traditional '20s look and centerpiece. Whole sets of dishes can sometimes be purchased very inexpensively and can provide a lifetime of enjoyment. Nice paper napkins and recyclable disposable

Vintage dishes with Five-Course Sandwich and Lower East Side Fermented Pickle

china are other options to make everything easy on the hosts. Or use your own dishes and snag just a couple of vintage serving pieces that you show-case to create the fun vibe you want.

ROARING TWENTIES MOVIES AND MUSIC

MAKE MOVIES A CO-STAR

Let the original stars of the big screen add a fun element to your party. The movie industry really blossomed during the 1920s. It was the rise of Hollywood. Consider how you can add a movie moment or several to your event or party if you feel like it. At the party itself, or even just as preparation to get you, your co-hosts, and guests in the mood.

> *"Those big movies around Fiftieth Street are cool," suggested Jordan. "I love New York on summer afternoons when everyone's away. There's something very sensuous about it—overripe, as if all sorts of funny fruits were going to fall into your hands."*

Here are a few ideas. Before the meal is served, run a movie in the background. It could be projected on a wall, on a big screen television, pull-up screen, or it could even appear on all visible device screens throughout the house, depending on your technology. You could also send out a few movie titles as recommendations for invited guests to explore, to get in the vibe before the party and build excitement. Or, for a private, stay-at-home event, show a movie as a family entertainment the night of your '20s party to complete the theme.

Movies of the 1920s were mostly silent. Some form of music always accompanied films, whether it was playing in the background or live music being played on a piano during the film. Slapstick comedy was popular, with hilarity and laughs delivered by actors like Charlie Chaplin, Buster Keaton, and Laurel and Hardy. Movie theaters were quite popular, with some of them holding up to two thousand people. The first talking-picture technology featuring synchronized sound, called the *talkie*, debuted in 1927 with the Warner Brothers film *The Jazz Singer*, featuring actor Al Jolson. It was also the first musical feature film. A huge accomplishment indeed, though it would now be recognized as racist, as might a number of movies from the era. Previewing and sensitivity are advised before suggesting or showing any of these movies.

There are numerous film versions of *The Great Gatsby*. The most recent was in 2013 starring Leonardo DiCaprio and Carey Mulligan. Earlier films were in 2000 with Toby Stephens and Mira Sorvino (made for TV). The 1974 classic starred Robert Redford and Mia Farrow. The 1949 version starred Alan Ladd and Betty Field. The very first version was a silent film starring Warner Baxter and Lois Wilson. It was made in 1926, just a year after the book was published. Only a one-minute clip of the trailer still exists.

For your consideration, here's a list of popular movies from the '20s:

- *The Last of the Mohicans* (1920 American silent film takes place in 1757 during the French and Indian War)
- *One Week* (1920 American silent comedy written by and starring Buster Keaton)
- *The Four Horsemen of the Apocalypse* (1921 American silent anti-war film starring Vicente Blasco Ibáñez, propelled Rudolph Valentino into stardom)
- *The Kid* (1921 silent comedy drama film written and debuting Charlie Chaplin about a man who finds a baby)
- *The Idle Class* (1921 American silent comedy film written and directed by Charlie Chaplin)
- *Orphans of the Storm* (1921 American silent drama during the French Revolution, directed by D. W. Griffith)
- *Cops* (1922 American silent comedy starring Buster Keaton about a young man who gets in trouble with the police)
- *The Hunchback of Notre Dame* (1923 American silent drama directed by Wallace Worsley, starring Lon Chaney)
- *Ten Commandments* (1923 silent religious epic film, directed by Cecil B. DeMille)
- *The Covered Wagon* (1923 American silent western directed by James Cruze)
- *The Wizard Of Oz* (The original 1925 silent fantasy-adventure version)

- *The Gold Rush* (1925 American silent comedy written by and starring Charlie Chaplin about the Klondike gold rush)
- *Phantom of the Opera* (1925 American silent horror film, directed by Rupert Julian)
- *The Big Parade* (1925 American silent war film directed by King Vidor)
- *Ben-Hur* (1925 American silent epic adventure-drama film directed by Fred Niblo, starring Ramon Novarro)
- *For Heaven's Sake* (1926 American silent comedy directed by Sam Taylor, starring Harold Lloyd)
- *What Price Glory?* (1926 American silent comedy war film directed by Raoul Walsh)
- *It* (1927 American silent romantic comedy, starring Clara Bow, thereafter dubbed "the It girl")
- *Wings* (1927 American silent war film, directed by William A. Wellman and starring Clara Bow, Charles Rogers, and Richard Arlen, takes place during World War I, Gary Cooper's small role in this film helped launch his career)
- *Metropolis* (1927 silent German expressionist science-fiction drama film, directed by Fritz Lang)
- *The Lodger: A Story of the London Fog* (1927 British silent thriller directed by Alfred Hitchcock)
- *Siren of the Tropics* (1927 French silent film starring Josephine Baker about a young Native girl in the West Indies who falls in love with a French man)
- *The Jazz Singer* (1927 American musical drama film directed by Alan Crosland and was the first major movie to use sound, triggering the end of the silent movie era)
- *Sunrise: A Song of Two Humans* (1927 American silent romantic drama)

- *The King of Kings* (1927 American silent epic film depicting Jesus in his last weeks before crucifixion, directed by Cecil B. DeMille)
- *The Passion of Joan of Arc* (1928 French silent historical film directed by Carl Theodor Dreyer about the trial of Joan d'Arc)
- *The Circus* (1928 American silent film written and starring Charlie Chaplin about a pickpocket and a circus)
- *The Road to Ruin* (1928 American silent exploitation film directed by Norton S. Parker, starring Helen Foster)
- *Abie's Irish Rose* (1928 part-talkie film directed by Victor Fleming)
- *L'Argent* (1928 French silent film directed by Marcel L'Herbier, about the stock market in Paris)
- *Speedy* (1928 American silent comedy film about a New York Yankees fan)
- *Ladies of the Mob* (1928 American silent crime drama directed by William A. Wellman is a gangster-themed romantic thriller)
- *Romance of the Underworld* (1928 American silent drama about flapper culture and the mob)
- *Sadie Thompson* (1928 American silent drama starring Gloria Swanson about a prostitute who meets a missionary)
- *The Cocoanuts* (1929 American pre-code talkie starring The Marx Brothers in their first movie)
- Piccadi*lly* (1929 British silent film directed by E.A. Dupont about a nightclub in London)
- *Blackmail* (1929 First British talkie film, directed by Alfred Hitchcock)
- *Pandora's Box* (1929 German silent film, starring Louise Brooks, about an alluring young woman who inspires lust and violence around her)

- *The Virginian* (1929 American Western talkie film directed by Victor Fleming and staring Gary Cooper. This was the first *talkie* film adapted from the 1902 novel of the same name)

For the silver screen's more modern take on the era, here are some movies set in the 1920s:

- *The Roaring Twenties* (1939 American crime thriller starring James Cagney and Humphrey Bogart about Prohibitionist America)
- *Singin' in the Rain* (1952 American musical starring Gene Kelly and Debbie Reynolds about the transition from silent films to talkies)
- *Some Like It Hot* (1959 American comedy starring Marilyn Monroe, Tony Curtis, and Jack Lemmon, takes place in 1929 Prohibition-era Chicago)
- *Thoroughly Modern Millie* (1967 American musical and romantic comedy film starring Julie Andrews about a young woman who comes to New York during the roaring twenties)
- *Bugsy Malone* (1976 American gangster musical comedy written by Alan Parker and starring Jodie Foster and Scott Baio, featuring child actors playing adult roles as a spoof on gangsters in New York and Chicago during Prohibition)
- *The Cotton Club* (1984 American crime drama co-written and directed by Francis Ford Coppola, centered around a Harlem jazz club in the late 1920s)
- *The Untouchables* (1987 American crime film directed by Brian De Palma, based on a book by David Mamet of the same name, starring Kevin Costner, Robert De Niro, and Sean Connery, about Al Capone and Eliot Ness during Prohibition in Chicago)
- *Chaplin* (1992 biographical comedy drama about the life of British comedian Charlie Chaplin, starring Robert Downey Jr, Marisa Tomei, Dan Aykroyd, Penelope Ann Miller, and Kevin Kline)

- *Bullets Over Broadway* (1994 American black comedy crime film directed by Woody Allen, starring John Cusack and Jennifer Tilly, takes place in 1928 New York about a struggling playwright)
- *The Cat's Meow* (2001 An international historical drama directed by Peter Bogdanovich and starring Kirsten Dunst, about the mysterious death of a film mogul in 1924)
- *Chicago* (2002 American musical crime comedy based on the 1975 stage musical of the same name, starring Renée Zellweger, Catherine Zeta-Jones, and Richard Gere, takes place in 1924 Chicago)
- *La Vie en Rose (Life in Pink)* (2007 International biographical musical about the life of French singer Edith Piaf)
- *Midnight in Paris* (2011 fantasy comedy-drama written and directed by Woody Allen, starring Owen Wilson and Rachel McAdams)
- *The Artist* (2011 French comedy drama, taking place in 1927 Hollywood, produced in the style of a silent film)

Remember, the goal is to have fun and enjoy yourself. Be flexible in your planning and willing to jettison ideas that sound fun but become cumbersome in making them happen easily. Try out your ideas and technology beforehand to make sure it all works together. A private moment with a delightful old movie to enjoy just for yourself might be much easier than adapting technology to include movies at your party. Stay open to possibilities while constantly taking care of yourself—a recipe for success!

DO YOU WANT TO DANCE?

Dancing in the '20s was a new frontier of freedom and personal expression. Most every town had places to gather and listen to dance bands. Venues like speakeasies, dance clubs, jazz clubs, and roadhouses popped up everywhere. There was an explosion of new dance styles that emerged with the growth of jazz. Some of the popular new styles included the Charleston, Shimmy, Chicken Scratch, Monkey Glide, Bunny Hug, Turkey Trot, Breakaway, Lindy Hop, Toddle, Kangaroo Hop, Castle Walk, and the outrageously sensual Tango.

> *There was dancing now on the canvas in the garden; old men pushing young girls backward in eternal graceless circles, superior couples holding each other tortuously, fashionably, and keeping in the corners—and a great number of single girls dancing individualistically or relieving the orchestra for a moment of the burden of the banjo or the traps. By midnight the hilarity had increased.*

The Lindy Hop was named after pilot Charles Lindbergh and was the first dance where men swung their partners into the air. First flight! Another fun fact: the popular '20s phrase *the bee's knees* was about a dancer. Though originally meaning something small and insignificant, the bee's knees came to mean something most excellent. That's because dancer Bee Jackson, who is credited with popularizing the Charleston, scandalously showed her knees while dancing. Her exposed knees were the talk of Broadway and beyond.

Many of these new dances required close physical contact between partners, which had previously been considered highly scandalous. Close dancing became the social norm. The moves were so energetic that many dance establishments featured "corset check rooms," where girls who might have left home wearing a corset could remove it before entering the dance hall.

Depending on your party, you may want to include time for dancing, perhaps even showing a video clip of a dancing lesson. There are plenty of easy-to-follow tutorials available on YouTube. Or you can make that part of your party prep: learn one dance from the era and have fun practicing it. Glide and shimmy, hop, and tango your way into your event. Show some gams, and be the bee's knee!

Suddenly one of these gypsies, in trembling opal, seizes a cocktail out of the air, dumps it down for courage and, moving her hands like Frisco, dances out alone on the canvas platform.

THE MUSIC OF THE JAZZ AGE

F. Scott Fitzgerald coined the term *The Jazz Age*, and his lifestyle and writings were the epitome of those times. The Jazz Age was much more than a new musical genre; it was a new way of living with a more liberated sense of self. It was an attitude, a behavior, an identity. It was artistic, rebellious, scandalous, flamboyant, and exciting! Jazz became associated with everything modern, sophisticated, classy, and decadent. Imagine flappers flapping all over the floor after checking their corsets at the door.

> *All night the saxophones wailed the hopeless comment of the "Beale Street Blues" while a hundred pairs of golden and silver slippers shuffled the shining dust. At the gray tea hour there were always rooms that throbbed incessantly with this low, sweet fever, while fresh faces drifted here and there like rose petals blown by the sad horns around the floor.*

Jazz originated in New Orleans in the early 1900s from the fusion of African, Anglo-American, and Creole influences. Although the first known recordings of jazz appeared in 1917, it skyrocketed to worldwide popularity in the '20s. It revolutionized the sound and structure of songs, making music livelier and much more deliriously danceable. Some considered jazz to be the devil's music, and there was plenty of heated public debate over it.

THE BIRTH OF THE CLUB CULTURE

Prohibition was the homemade rocket fuel that ignited the underground club culture. Jazz was king. Speakeasies became highly competitive, with owners, many of whom were bootleggers and mobsters, competing for the best performers. The club culture craze fueled the evolution of jazz.

Louis Armstrong is considered the most influential musician in the history of jazz. Other pioneering players include Duke Ellington, Sidney Bechet, and Benny Goodman. Jazz and the availability of gigs created a sense of integration between Black and white in the industry. It provided a newfound upward, social mobility among Black jazz musicians and offered entry into the deep, rich, Black music roots for white musicians. Everyone benefitted. Iconic nightclubs in New York's Harlem District were The Cotton Club, The Apollo, and Connie's Inn.

Jazz growth was dramatically driven by the advent of radio. The first commercial radio stations began broadcasting in 1920, with more than five hundred and fifty radio stations operating across the nation within just two years, all sending out the magic of jazz to play across the airwaves.

Technological advances drove the growth of jazz: coin-operated phonographs, which was the predecessor of the jukebox, player pianos, and band instrument machines were found in many speakeasies.

Jazz up your party with some of these tunes:

- "Wang Wang Blues" (1920) Henry Busse, Gussie Mueller, and Theron E. "Buster" Johnson; lyrics by Leo Wood
- "Margie" (1920) Con Conrad, J. Russel Robinson, and Benny Davis
- "The Sheik of Araby" (1921) Ted Snyder, Harry B. Smith, and Frances Wheeler
- "Wabash Blues" (1921) Fred Meinken and Dave Ringle/ Isham Jones

- "Beale Street Blues" (1921) W.C. Handy (Marion Harris)
- "Bugle Call Rag" (1922) Billy Meyers, Jack Pettis, and Elmer Schoebel
- "Farewell Blues" (1922) Paul Mares, Leon Roppolo, and Elmer Schoebel
- "I Wish I Could Shimmy Like My Sister Kate" (1922) Armand J. Piron
- "Tin Roof Blues" (1923) George Brunies, Paul Mares, Ben Pollack, Leon Roppolo, and Mel Stitzel
- "Aggravatin' Papa (Don't You Try to Two-Time Me)" (1923) Bessie Smith (Foxtrot)
- "The Original Charleston" (1923) James P. Johnson and R. C. McPherson
- "Linger Awhile" (1923) Vincent Rose and Harry Owens
- "Rhapsody in Blue" (1924) Paul Whiteman/George Gershwin
- "Dinah" (1925) Harry Akst, Sam M. Lewis and Joe Young/ Ethel Waters
- "Muskrat Ramble" (1926) Kid Ory/Louis Armstrong
- "Heebie Jeebies" (1926) Boyd Atkins/Louis Armstrong
- "That Sugar Baby o' Mine" (1926) Maceo Pinkard, Edna Alexander, and Sidney D. Mitchell/Ethel Waters
- "I've Found A New Baby" (1926) Ted Lewis/Ethel Waters
- "I Ain't Got Nobody" (1926) Marion Harris/Sophie Tucker / Bessie Smith
- "'Deed I Do" (1926) Fred Rose and Walter Hirsch/Benny Goodman
- "Sleepy Time Gal" (1926) Ben Bernie/Gene Austin/Nick Lucas
- "Big Butter and Egg Man" (1926) Percy Venable/Louis Armstrong (May Alix)

- "In A Mist" (1927) Bix Beiderbecke
- "Black and Tan Fantasy" (1927) Duke Ellington and Bubber Miley
- "East St. Louis Toodle-oo" (1927) Duke Ellington and Bubber Miley
- "Singin' the Blues" (1927) Frankie Trumbauer, Bix Beiderbecke, and Eddie Lang
- "Makin' Whoopee" (1928) Gus Kahn and Walter Donaldson/ Eddie Cantor/Paul Whiteman (Bing Crosby)
- "Doin' the Racoon" (1928) J. Fred Coots and Raymond Klages/ George Olsen/The Knickerbockers/Rudy Vallée
- "Happy Days and Lonely Nights" (1928) Billy Rose and Fred Fisher/The Harmony Brothers/Ruth Etting
- "Sweet Lorraine" (1928) Cliff Burwell and Mitchell Parish
- "West End Blues" (1928) Louis Armstrong
- "Ain't Misbehavin'" (1929) Fats Waller, Harry Brooks, and Andy Razaf/Louis Armstrong

MAKE IT POP!

Popular music in the 1920s was easy-going, carefree, and lively, with catchy melodies and simple harmonies. Much of it was created by a group of music songwriters and publishers in New York City, known as Tin Pan Alley.

Some of these songs may be surprisingly familiar to you. They have been remade many times over the years. How many have you heard before?

Though *The Great Gatsby* is set in 1922, any of these songs from the '20s will help set the mood:

- "Swanee" (1920) George Gershwin and Irving Caesar/Al Jolson
- "Avalon" (1920) Al Jolson, Buddy DeSylva, and Vincent Rose
- "The Dardanella Blues" (1920) Johnny S. Black and Fred Fisher
- "When My Baby Smiles at Me" (1920) Bill Munro, Andrew B. Sterling, and Ted Lewis
- "Whispering" (1920) John Schonberger and Malvin Schonberger
- "Saloon" (1921) Ernest R. Ball and George Whiting
- "Second Hand Rose" (1921) James F. Hanley and Grant Clarke/ Fanny Brice
- "April Showers" (1921) Al Jolson and Buddy DeSylva
- "Ain't We Got Fun" (1921) Richard A. Whiting, Raymond B. Egan, Danny Russo, and Gus Kahn/Van & Schenck
- "California, Here I Come" (1921) Buddy DeSylva and Joseph Meyer/Al Jolson
- "Toot, Toot, Tootsie (Goo'bye)" (1922) Gus Kahn, Ernie Erdman, and Al Jolson
- "You've Got to See Mamma Ev'ry Night" (1923) Con Conrad and Billy Rose

- "Barney Google" (1923) Con Conrad and Billy Rose
- "It Ain't Gonna Rain No Mo'" (1923) Wendell Hall
- "Yes! We Have No Bananas" (1923) Frank Silver and Irving Cohn/Eddie Cantor/Billy Jones/Ben Selvin
- "Rhapsody in Blue" (1924) George Gershwin
- "Fascinating Rhythm" (1924) George Gershwin and Ira Gershwin
- "The Prisoner's Song" (1924) Vernon Dalhart, Guy Massey
- "It Had to Be You" (1924) Isham Jones and Gus Kahn/Marion Harris
- "Bye Bye Blackbird" (1924) Jerome H. Remick, Ray Henderson, and Mort Dixon/Gene Austin/Nick Lucas
- "Yes Sir, That's My Baby" (1925) Walter Donaldson and Gus Kahn
- "Show Me the Way to Go Home" (1925) Jimmy Campbell and Reg Connelly (Irving King)
- "Five Foot Two, Eyes of Blue (Has Anybody Seen My Gal?" (1925) Ray Henderson, Sam M. Lewis, and Joseph Widow Young/The California Ramblers/Gene Austin
- "If You Knew Susie (Like I Know Susie!)" (1925) Buddy DeSylva and Joseph Meyer/Eddie Cantor/Cliff Edwards/Al Jolson
- "Sweet Georgia Brown" (1925) Ben Bernie, Maceo Pinkard, and Kenneth Casey
- "I Never See Maggie Alone" (1926) Everett Lynton and Harry Tilsley
- "Baby Face" (1926) Benny Davis and Harry Akst
- "Someone to Watch Over Me" (1926) George Gershwin and Ira Gershwin
- "Doctor Jazz" (1926) Joe "King" Oliver
- "I'm Looking Over a Four Leaf Clover" (1927) Harry Woods and Mort Dixon

- "Ol' Man River" (1927) Jerome Kern and Oscar Hammerstein II
- "My Blue Heaven" (1927) Walter Donaldson and George A. Whiting/Gene Austin
- "Me and My Shadow" (1927) Al Jolson, Billy Rose, and Dave Dreyer/ "Whispering" Jack Smith/Nat Shilkret
- "Crazy Rhythm" (1928) Joseph Meyer, Roger Wolfe Kahn, and Irving Caesar
- "Sonny Boy" (1928) Ray Henderson, Buddy De Sylva, and Lew Brown/Al Jolson
- "My Man (Mon Homme)" (1928) Maurice Yvain, Jacques-Charles, and Abert Willemetz/Fanny Brice
- "I'm Wild About Horns on Automobiles That Go 'Ta Ta Ta Ta'" (1928) Clarence Gaskill
- I Wanna Be Loved by You (1928) Herbert Stothart, Harry Ruby, and Bert Kalmar/Helen Kane
- "Let's Do It (Let's Fall in Love)" (1928) Cole Porter/Dorsey Brothers Orchestra (Bing Crosby)/Rudy Vallée
- "Honey" (1929) Seymour Simons, Haven Gillespie, and Richard A. Whiting/Rudy Vallée
- "Puttin' on the Ritz" (1929) Irving Berlin
- "Am I Blue?" (1929) Harry Akst and Grant Clarke/Ethel Waters/ Libby Holman/Annette Hanshaw
- "Tiptoe Through the Tulips" (1929) Al Dubin and Joe Burke/ Nick Lucas
- "Singin' in The Rain" (1929) Nacio Herb Brown and Arthur Freed

THE BIRTH OF THE BLUES

The '20s welcomed the birth of the blues, which originated from the creative influences of Black culture and heritage. Blues was the music of the people, not of the professional songwriters. Lyrics came from life experience and from the heart. Mamie Smith was the first Black artist to make a blues recording. She was a well-known vaudeville performer and hit the big time after recording "Crazy Blues" in 1921. In 1927, Smith became the highest-paid Black artist in the world. She was the first Black singer to sell over a million records.

Add a taste of the blues to your party play list:

- "It's Right Here for You (If You Don't Get It, 'Tain't No Fault o' Mine)" (1920) Perry Bradford/Mamie Smith
- "Crazy Blues" (1921) Perry Bradford/Mamie Smith
- "That Thing Called Love" (1921) Perry Bradford/Mamie Smith
- "You Can't Keep a Good Man Down" (1921) Perry Bradford/ Mamie Smith
- "Downhearted Blues" (1923) Alberta Hunter and Lovie Austin/ Bessie Smith
- "'Tain't Nobody's Biz-Ness If I Do" (1923) Porter Grainger and Everett Robbins/Bessie Smith
- "Nobody Knows When You're Down and Out" (1923) Jimmie Cox/Bessie Smith
- "See See Rider Blues" (1924) Ma Rainey
- "Shake That Thing" (1925) Ethel Waters/Papa Charlie Jackson
- "St. Louis Blues" (1925) W.C. Handy/Bessie Smith/Louis Armstrong/Marion Harris
- "James Alley Blues" (1927) Richard "Rabbit" Brown

- "Dark Was the Night, Cold Was the Ground" (1927) Blind Willie Johnson
- "Statesboro Blues" (1928) Blind Willie McTell
- "Empty Bed Blues" (1928) J.C. Johnson/Bessie Smith

ADD A DASH OF COUNTRY

English, Scottish, and Irish settlers living in the southern Appalachian Mountains brought us country music, originally called *hillbilly* music, back in the 1920s. The Carter Family was the first vocal group to become country music stars and were very influential throughout the decade. Talk about a family legacy! Hillbilly music caught on quickly, leading to the founding of the beloved The Grand Ole Opry in Nashville, Tennessee, in November 1925.

If you want to get your hillbilly on and add some country twang, here are some suggestions:

- "Lovesick Blues" (1922) Emmett Miller & His Georgia Crackers
- "Little Log Cabin in the Lane" (1923) "Fiddlin'" John Carson
- "Don't Let Your Deal Go Down Blues" (1925) Charlie Poole
- If I Could Be with You (One Hour Tonight) (1926) James P. Johnson and Henry Creamer
- "Blue Yodel No. 1 (T for Texas)" (1927) Jimmie Rodgers
- "Matchbox Blues" (1927) Blind Lemon Jefferson
- "Fishing Blues" (1928) Henry Thomas
- "In the Jailhouse Now" (1928) Jimmie Rodgers
- "The Brakeman's Blues" (1928) Jimmie Rodgers
- "Wildwood Flower" (1928) The Carter Family
- "Keep on the Sunny Side of Life" (1928) The Carter Family
- "Down on Penny's Farm" (1929) The Bentley Boys
- "Waiting for a Train" (1929) Jimmie Rodgers

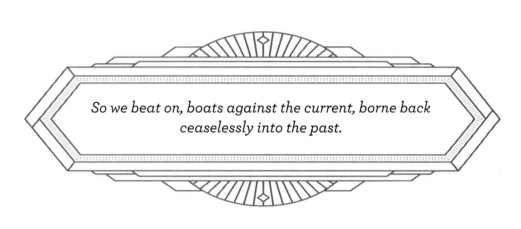

So we beat on, boats against the current, borne back ceaselessly into the past.

HANDY MEASUREMENT
CONVERSION CHART

1 GALLON
4 QUARTS
8 PINTS
16 CUPS
128 OUNCES
3.8 LITERS

1 QUART
2 PINTS
4 CUPS
32 OUNCES
950 ML

1 PINT
2 CUPS
16 OUNCES
480 ML

1 CUP
16 TBSP
8 OUNCES
240 ML

1/2 CUP
8 TBSP
4 OUNCES
120 ML

1/4 CUP
4 TBSP
2 OUNCES
60 ML

1 OUNCE
2 TBSP
30 ML

1 TBLSP
3 TSP
1/2 OUNCE
15 ML

1 TSP
5 ML

GRATITUDE AND APPRECIATION

Putting this book together truly took a village and we are most appreciative of all of the love and support received!

All italicized quotes throughout the book are from *The Great Gatsby* by F. Scott Fitzgerald. The text of the original book is in the public domain.

Marshall Williams was the brilliant photographer who shot the food photo assemblages, individual recipe items, the Gatsby plate, plus the photos of Chef Ron. Contact Marshall at www.MarshallWilliams.com.

Vast waves of appreciation and gratitude to our editor extraordinaire Melissa Morgan. Thanks to the wonderful folks at Post Hill Press including Anthony Ziccardi, Megan Wheeler, Debra Englander, Heather King, Cody Corcoran, Sara Ann Alexander, and Alana Mills, plus the entire team.

Thank you to Chef Amanda Grotewiel for your contributions to the recipe development, recipe testing, and photo shoot. Isabel Oliver was a constant source of support, encouragement, and brilliant ideas. Thank you!

Bertha Edington was our fashion correspondent and Paula Wansley put together the movie and music suggestions. Thanks to Rick Smith, Darity Wesley, Ingrid Coffin, and Bill Jurel.

A big shout out to The Mob Museum in Las Vegas for the Speakeasy photos from The Underground. Photos by Chris Wessling. Check them out at www.TheMobMuseum.org. Tell 'em Gatsby sent you.

Thank you to the San Diego community for your generosity in lending us treasured items for our photo shoot. Luis Garcia served as digital tech.

The marvelous Melissa Morgan served as our antique expert and property mistress. Linda Hanover generously loaned us a treasure trove of items to include. Thank you! Dave McPheeters of Zac's Attic in San Diego also provided some of the items and expertise. Melissa also thanks Mission Gallery, Randle Batley, and Dee Dee Varner for lots of running around, demitasse tea cups, and general help, plus Heidi Fleischbein for providing the tiered tea tray.

Cristina had a vision of a trumpet in the speakeasy photo. Melissa asked Lisa Tansey, who suggested Armand Frigon, who put out the call. A big fanfare and shout out to all the musicians who helped us get brassy including Lee Fugal, Nightshade Navarro, Dennis McKinley, and highlighted trumpet donor Jon Roussos.

Chef Ron was very touched by the generosity of three people for allowing us to borrow their cherished items for the photo shoot. Kathy Taylor contributed many items including a set of china that her grandmother received as a wedding gift in the 1920s and another set that her other grandmother actually hand-painted herself in the same decade. Susan Barnes Johnson lent some incredible etched liquor bottles, salt and pepper shakers, other tableware, and the copper mold we used for the Strawberry Bavarian. Nancy Atherton West lent us an amazing and functioning 1920s typewriter along with some other service pieces.

Additional images were created by many talented artists globally and licensed on Dreamstime.com. Model licenses are included in the Dreamstime license.

ABOUT THE AUTHORS

Chef Ron Oliver

Award-winning chef and author Ron Oliver has been researching the history of food and gastronomy since he was a teenager. Fascinated by everything from the diet of the ancient Incas to the global diaspora of Portuguese culinary traditions, to the different periods of the modern American kitchen, he jumped at the chance to join the "Gatsby Cookbook Team" and create a 1920s menu that would be true to the era.

A dedicated chef, he believes that the kitchen is not only about making food, but creating memories and bringing happiness to people's lives. Ron has traveled to far reaches of the world in search of culinary inspiration. Back in his own home kitchen, he seeks out the finest local, natural, and fresh ingredients to star in his tasty creations. Ron's unique talent is to blend the exotic ingredients and preparations discovered through his research into signature dishes that surprise and delight the palate.

Chef Ron's first cookbook, the celebrated *Flying Pans* with Chef Bernard Guillas, earned the IACP Cookbook of the Year. He was named Chef of the Year by the San Diego Chapter of the California Restaurant Association in 2017 and, as former Chef de Cuisine of the prestigious Marine Room in La Jolla, California, Ron led his talented team to eight titles as Best Restaurant in San Diego. He teaches cooking classes, caters special occasion events, and is a chef consultant for start-up and existing restaurants.

Chef Ron's passion for food and cooking expands to support local schools and to help young people learn about food literacy by planting sustainable gardens. The idea that food is a gift from the earth, that cooking is an act of love, and that eating is socially unifying, are all concepts he learned in the kitchen.

Other books by Ron Oliver:

Flying Pans: Two Chefs, One World with Chef Bernard Guillas

Two Chefs, One Catch: A Culinary Exploration of Seafood with Chef Bernard Guillas

Contact Chef Ron at www.ChefRonOliver.com

Cristina Smith

Award-winning author of the *Yoga for the Brain* series, Cristina Smith loves to play with her food. She approaches cooking as an artform. Cristina believes that food is fun and a gift. A culinary creation is a wonderful way share love, health, and beauty in a personal way. Cooking is an immediate art because once it's gone, it's done. There's nothing to store except maybe leftovers. Then the food artist can begin afresh with a new palette of ingredients for inspiration.

Cristina cut her culinary teeth as a member of the iconic Big Kitchen catering team, founded by San Diego community leader, Judy "The Beauty on Duty" Forman. Later, she served as Executive Chef for Blue Sky Ranch community and retreat center for fifteen years. Cristina delighted event attendees with healthy, beautiful, delicious, and unexpectedly magical meals that regularly brought them back for more.

Cristina and Ron met when he began ordering produce from Blue Sky Ranch for the Marine Room around the turn of the century. They share a love of living a delicious life, and developed a friendship over the years. Ron mentored Cristina's son as a chef, and Cristina mentored Ron's daughter as an author.

Other books by Cristina Smith include:

Life Wisdom Word Search: Yoga for the Brain with Rick Smith and 60 Contributing Authors

Inspired Wisdom Word Search: Yoga for the Brain with Rick Smith and 60 Contributing Authors

Animal Wisdom Word Search: Yoga for the Brain with Rick Smith and Lauren McCall

The Word Search Sage: Yoga for the Brain with Rick Smith and Ingrid Coffin

The Word Search Oracle: Yoga for the Brain with Rick Smith and Darity Wesley

The Tao of Sudoku: Yoga for the Brain with Rick Smith

Contact Cristina at www.YogaForTheBrain.com

Chef Ron and Cristina had a deliciously delightful time collaborating on this book. They wish all readers the joy of cooking!

Cheers!